THE SECRET WISDOM OF THE QABALAH

A Study in Jewish Mystical Thought

By

J. F. C. FULLER

Unabridged Edition

Created by, Z. El-Bey

"The Beings who live Below, say that God is on High; while the Angels in Heaven, say that God is on Earth."-ZOHAR.

Ordering Information:

Quantity sales. Special discounts are available on quantity purchases by corporations, associations, and others. For details, contact the publisher at the address above.

Orders by U.S. trade bookstores and wholesalers. Please contact us at ilifeebooks@gmail.com

Printed in the United States of America

THE SECRET WISDOM
OF THE QABALAH

A Study in Jewish Mystical Thought

By

J. F. C. FULLER

NADA	AIN 66
NADA SIN LIMITES	AIN SUPH
LUZ ILIMITADA	AIN SUPH AUR

1 CORONA	1 KETHER
2 SABIDURIA	2 CHOKMAH
3 ENTENDIMIENTO	3 BINAH
4 CONOCIMIENTO	4 DAÄTH
4 MISERICORDIA	4 CHESED
5 SEVERIDAD	5 GEBURAH
6 BELLEZA	6 TIPHARETH
7 VICTORIA	7 NETZACH
8 ESPLENDOR	8 HOD
9 FUNDAMENTO	9 YESOD
10 REINO	10 MALKUTH
11 BUEY	11 ALEPH
12 CASA	12 BETH
13 CAMELLO	13 GIMEL
14 PUERTA	14 DALETH
15 VENTANA	15 HEH
16 CLAVO	16 VAV
17 ESPADA	17 ZAIN
18 CERCA	18 CHETH
19 SERPIENTE	19 TETH
20 MANO ABIERTA	20 YOD
21 MANO CERRADA	21 KAPH
22 AGUIJON	22 LAMED
23 MARES	23 MEM
24 PEZ	24 NUN
25 SOPORTE	25 SAMECH
26 OJO	26 AYIN
27 BOCA	27 PEH
28 ANZUELO	28 TZADDY
29 CABEZA (POSTERIOR)	29 QOPH
30 ROSTRO	30 RESH
31 DIENTE	31 SHIN
32 TAU O CRUZ	32 TAU

K TANKIGU ELEMENTO

CONTENTS

AGNZ

PREFACE

This small book is in no sense a treatise on the Qabalah. Instead, it is a speculative study on one of several secret doctrines which it contains, and, I believe, the key-doctrine of all the others. Should this be correct, then it follows that, unless this doctrine is understood, the whole symbolism of Jewish mysticism must remain obscure, and it is this mysticism, so it seems to me, which constitutes the foundations of Jewish culture and Jewish aspirations.

Granted that this is so, then it follows that the idea elaborated in this book is one of considerable importance, even if many of my interpretations are faulty. Even if the whole of my readings are wrong, which is unlikely, this in itself does not necessarily invalidate the idea. For example: Columbus believed that the world was round and he set out to prove it. In doing so he discovered a new world, which, though it did not at the time actually confirm this idea, established a stepping-stone to the circumnavigation of the globe, which did confirm it in an obvious and uncontradictable way.

So also in this book, I have set out to penetrate the mists of Qabalistic learning, not because I presume to be an adept in its mysteries, but because I suspect that they hide within them the idea of a new world conception, an idea which for 2000 years has been struggling to take form. Should I be right in this belief, then it follows that once this form consolidates from out of it will emanate a new ideology, which will exert so stupendous an influence upon our lives that it will constitute a world revolution. Nevertheless, I do not intend to touch upon this possibility in the present work; for all I will attempt is to show that the idea is valid. Therefore my object is solely to examine and explain it, in order to establish it as a fact.

J. F. C. F.

LIST OF ILLUSTRATIONS

PLATES

DIAGRAMS

INTRODUCTION

The Mystical Foundations of the World Order.

Life is shrouded in a mystery; this is the fundamental fact which confronts us. We live in a cave with our backs to the light, and, as Plato said, our knowledge is nothing more than the shadows which play upon its walls.

What this mystery is in itself we cannot tell. All we know is that it exists, and ultimately all we know of ourselves is that we exist. If we call this mystery "God", then our lives vibrate between the two poles of "God is" and "I am"; but because the first transcends the reason, as the infinite transcends the finite, the relationship between them can only be expressed in symbols; that is in finite, or rational, terms. If in the place of God we write "Reality", "Nature", "Unknowable", or "Zero", it matters not one whit; the equation is just as obscure; for all we have done is to replace *a* by *b*, *c*, *d*, or *e*, not knowing what these letters mean. The symbol has changed, but what it symbolizes remains as inscrutable.

Granted that this is so, then it follows that our intellectual lives are purely symbolical existences. All our thoughts are nothing more than symbols of a mystery, whether it embraces God - the ultimate source of all things - or reality - the tangible world in which we live. All are, in fact, equidistant from what they represent and are, consequently, of equal value from the point of view of the represented. If say that "God is ineffable", "God is inscrutable", or "God is omnipotent", though the words differ we are saying no more than that "God is". All these word symbols are of equal value, because they in no way uncover this mystery. Yet, though equidistant from the represented, these symbols are by no means equidistant from the mind of man, which is not archetypal but protean; that is to say it is for ever changing its intellectual forms. Whilst at one time one set of symbols keeps it in tune with the mystery, at another time a different set of symbols can alone do so. Consequently, though *a*, *b*, *c*, *d*, and *e* are all of equal value to the represented, they are by no means of equal value to the representer - ourselves.

Granted that this is so, then it follows that symbols, to remain potent, must change as intellectual concepts change. For example, should we today declare that the universe is composed of minute indivisible and indestructible atoms of matter, we can expect no appeal from. the scientific mind; because the conception of the universe has changed and the man of science is thinking in terms of electrical waves or waves of light. Nevertheless, these waves are just as much symbols as atoms are, and in themselves they explain nothing; yet their virtue lies in that they fit better into the present order of scientific thought; that is - symbolically they are not out of place.

As long as they maintain their place they maintain their attractive power by bringing the mind into contact with the mystery; and so long as this contact endures an equilibrium is established between the mystery and the intelligence, and the mind is held, as it were in a state of wonder - that is of love or attraction. So long as this equilibrium lasts, - that is so long as faith in the potency of the symbol is overwhelming - contentedness monopolizes the life of man; but directly this faith declines, discontent intervenes, and it is in discontent that must be sought the origins of all world revolutions.

Why is this so? Because the finite can only find succour in the infinite, the potent in the omnipotent, the limited in the unlimited, the mortal in the immortal, the child in the mother. Cut away the greater, and the lesser is bereft of hope. It is like a ship drifting on a shoreless sea. She may be well built, well stocked, and bravely manned, yet her destiny is foreordained; having no port to put into, sooner or later she and her crew must sink beneath the waters and be lost for ever.

When this doom encompasses mankind, as today it would seem to encompass it, man does not so much wring his hands in despair as drown his hopelessness in physical enjoyments. "Let us eat and drink. ... for tomorrow we die" become the passwords of the age, and the more this obsession gains sway the less does wonder illumine his path, until the age enters its eclipse. Love becomes lust, the noble ignoble, the beautiful hideous, the generous selfish, and all is lost in a scramble of greed's. It is in this dismal darkness that Satan materializes and Satanism becomes a cult. The symbols go on, potent and impotent; but now they are turned upside down, for fear is hope reversed.

What causes this vacuum into which fear rushes? A breakdown in the equilibrium between the mysterious and the intelligible. As there is the greater mystery between God and the mind of man, so also is there the lesser mystery between mind and the body of mankind. The knowing are few; the ignorant are many. What to the one is supreme goodness, to the other may prove to be a deadly poison. As Adam eating of the Tree of the Knowledge of Good and Evil lost Eden, so throughout the ages have the wise kept wisdom to themselves, imparting to the multitudes only just sufficient knowledge to fill them with wonder, and guarding against giving too much lest wonder intoxicates them and turns them mad. When this wisdom has been observed an equilibrium has been established in the social order, and when it has not been observed chaos has always held sway. A society or a civilization seldom perishes by the sword; nearly always it perishes through a defamation of the mysteries which held it in equilibrium. When Ham uncovered his father's nakedness he was cursed; so also was Prometheus punished for stealing fire from heaven. Thus it happens that a people or a civilization is cursed when its rulers uncover the mysteries in the public places. When the symbols are made cheap they are misunderstood, they cease to be symbolical and become real, idols in the eyes of the multitudes. When the multitudes dance round the Golden Calf, then are the Tables of the Law cast upon the ground.

All this may seem strange to us today, when everything is trumpeted abroad and sold for gold and there is no righteousness in the land; when love and lust, sorrow, tragedy, and excitement are sold for a penny in the newspapers, and when all that is sacred and vicious is broadcasted around for much less. The exploitation of the mysteries is the order of this age; there is no secrecy except that of exaggeration and untruthfulness. Yet may not it be said: Is not the progress of to-day due almost entirely to publicity? Yes, that is undoubted; but what profits progress if the world is to be filled with discontent? Freedom is a sublime mystery, but when this mystery is vulgarized it becomes anarchy. Look around: everywhere we see turmoil, strife, jealousy, fear, and greed; Satan brooding over the four corners of the world and the drums of war beating nearer and nearer.

Behind this turmoil crouches the Machine, the Baphomet of the age of iron. He should have been the servant of man, yet he has become his master. He should have mitigated the curse of Eden and have transformed toil and labor into leisure and contentment. Why has he failed to do so? Because the mysteries of physical science, having slipped the leash of secrecy, have, like maenads, coursed madly about the world. Once the searchers after the mysteries of Nature worked in a gloom of fear, locking away their knowledge in ciphers and cryptograms; now they stride into their laboratories seeking to transmute knowledge into gold, and when the people cannot understand their jargon they fall back upon the pen of the novel-writer, transforming scientific fact into romantic fiction.

Why has science thus failed us? Because the wisdom of the few has been cast like pearls before the swinish ignorance of the many. The intellectual evolution of the masses has not kept pace with the physical evolution of the scientists. A new body has been built, a body of titanic power, yet it is still inhabited by a mind which belongs to a far less powerful instrument. The result is a moral disintegration - a throwing out of balance, out of focus, out of equilibrium. Chaos surrounds us, because the mysteries have been communicated to those unworthy to receive them, and not until the new body is endowed with a new mind will a new soul be born within it. Such an equilibrium can alone be established through wonder - a stepping out from the finite towards the infinite, a transmutation of Satan into God.

The Secrecy of Transcendental Knowledge

Transcendental knowledge is knowledge which transcends the intelligence, yet it need not therefore be knowledge which is beyond the focus of the mind. The differential calculus is common knowledge to the mathematician, and yet it is transcendental to the majority of mankind. So also with practically all science; it is in itself the perquisite of the few whom we call the wise. Today the fundamental difference between the science of this age and the science of past ages is that, whilst formerly the universe was looked upon as being full of symbols which, when read correctly, could lead us to the Real Being which they clothed, today the universe is considered to be Reality itself, a tangible being, a something which exists *separated* from us and which we can probe with our physical senses and take apart and put together again as if it were a machine. The mystical conception has been replaced by the mechanical conception, and yet in itself the mystery remains as profound.

Christ understood this when He said: "Give not that which is holy unto the dogs, neither cast ye your pearls before swine, lest they trample them under their feet, and turn again and rend you."[1] To the common folk Christ spoke in parables, not because He was of a common mind, but because He was an initiate and so understood how fine is the division between reason and madness, and how easily can knowledge dissolve the filament which separates these two. This essential wisdom, and wisdom is largely the application of knowledge to circumstances, has always been realized in the East. Amongst the Jews, and Christ was of that race, we find it firmly established, and it is not a mere coincidence that the Hebrew word *Sod*, which means "mystery" or "secrets", has the same numerical value, namely 70, as the Hebrew word which represents "wine"; for mystery can intoxicate as well as refresh.

The mysteries of the early Hebrews were closely guarded by the Sons of the Doctrine, and it would appear that many of their secrets were derived from Egypt and later on from Babylonia. We are told that Moses was learned in all the wisdom of the Egyptians[2] and that in the first four books of the Pentateuch he has esoterically laid down the principles of the secret doctrine. He initiated seventy elders into the mysteries,[3] which they transmitted from mouth to ear. Generally speaking, the initiates led an ascetic life in order to separate themselves from the ignorant and unwise, so that they might guard against divulging their doctrines.

In these distant days the mysteries of Nature, and what is now called physical science, formed part of the hidden cult. Thus Pythagoras, Anaximander, Nicetas, Heraclides, Aristarchus, Seleneus, and Ecphantus believed in the rotundity of the earth or in its movement; the first of these philosophers holding that each star was a world possessing its own atmosphere and surrounded by immense spaces of ether.[4] But this knowledge was never popularized for fear of upsetting religion, by means of which authority over the ignorant masses was maintained. Early in the fourth century A.D. we find Lactantius writing:

It is an absurdity to believe that there are men who have feet above their heads, and countries in which all is inverted, in which the trees and plants grow from the top to the bottom. We find the germ of that error among the philosophers who have claimed that the earth is round.[5]

St. Augustine held a similar opinion.[6] Long before Copernicus wrote his book, *Revolution of the Heavenly Bodies* (about A.D. 1542), we find that the medieval Jews had buried this secret in the *Zohar*, in which may be read:

In the book of Hammannunah the Old we learn . . . that the earth turns upon itself in the form of a circle; that some are on top, and others below; that all creatures change in aspect, following the manner of each place, keeping however in the same position, but there are some countries of the earth which are lightened, whilst others are in darkness; these have the day when for the former it is night; and there are countries in which it is constantly day, or in which at least the night continues only some instants. . . . These secrets were made known to the men of the secret science but not to the geographers.[7]

Though refuted by Origen,[8] Celsus was undoubtedly right when he declared that the primitive Christian Church was possessed of a secret system, and Weishaupt, the supposed founder of the Illuminati, may not have been altogether wrong when he said:

No one . . . has so cleverly concealed the high meaning of His teaching, and no one finally has so surely and easily directed men on to the path of freedom, as our great master Jesus of Nazareth. This secret meaning and natural consequence of His teaching He hid completely, for Jesus had a secret doctrine, as we see in more than one place of the Scriptures.[9]

Whether this is so or not, there can be no doubt whatever that the Bible is a mystical work containing a secret doctrine which is only known to those who have been initiated into it. What part of this doctrine is will be discovered later on in this book.

From this brief excursion into the past it will be seen that secrecy has played an important part in human history. The idea that all knowledge should be divulged and broadcast among the masses is something quite modern. Even as late as the seventeenth century, when Leibnitz published in the *Acta Eruditorum* of Leipzig his scheme of differential calculus, he did so in such a way as to hide both the method and object from the uninitiated. Newton did the same with his invention of infinite series; and algebra, as far as it was understood by the Arabians, was, as a secret, known to and hidden by certain Italian mathematicians for three hundred years.

The Jewish Secret Doctrines

The world is a mystery, and mysteries are dangerous to the uninitiated: here are two facts which would seem to be uncontradictable; for divulgence has invariably led to active discontent, caused by a loss of balance between the spiritual and the mundane.

Like all other peoples, the Jews realized this, and long before the Qabalah was known as an occult science, the mysteries of creation, evolution, and dissolution were locked up in their sacred writings. Then came the great dispersion: a small people bereft of nationship was cast into a dissolving world, and almost simultaneously a new cult arose called Christianity - a Jewish heresy. The reaction on orthodox Jewry was instantaneous; for a tension was established which later on led to the persecution of the Jews, whereupon the secrecy of the doctrines took on an accentuated form, for self-preservation had now to be added to non-revelation. This led to the growth of oral traditions. The secret doctrines were passed from mouth to mouth and were locked away in the brains of the priesthood and the learned. Later, as persecution began to slacken, the written word once again began to appear, and by degrees the Qabalah emerged into daylight.

This word is a curious one: its value is 70, which is, as we have seen, the numerical value of *Sod* (dvs = 4+6+60) and "wine" (Oyy = 50 + 10 + 10) and also of "night" (l yl = 30 + 10 + 30) and "be silent" (hs h = 5 + 6o + 5). Therefore it may be said to mean: "The secret which intoxicates, which is as dark as night and which must not be divulged."

The fountain-head of this doctrine is the *Zohar*, or *Book of Splendour*, a vast jumbled commentary on the Pentateuch, written partly in Aramaic and partly in Hebrew. Tradition asserts that its author was Rabbi Simeon ben Yohai, who lived in the second century A.D.; of it Ginsburg says:

It was first taught by God himself to a select company of angels, who formed a theosophic school in Paradise. After the fall the angels most graciously communicated this heavenly doctrine to the disobedient child of earth, to furnish the protoplasts with the means of returning to their pristine nobility and felicity. From Adam it passed over to Noah, and then to Abraham, the friend of God, who immigrated with it to Egypt, where the patriarch allowed a portion of this mysterious doctrine to ooze out. It was in this way that the Egyptians obtained some knowledge of it, and the other eastern nations could introduce it into their philosophical systems. Moses, who was learned in all the wisdom of Egypt, was first initiated into it in the land of his birth, but became most proficient in it during his wanderings in the wilderness, when he not only devoted to it the leisure hours of the whole forty years, but received lessons in it from one of the angels. By the aid of this mysterious science the lawgiver was enabled to solve the difficulties which arose during his management of the Israelites, in spite of the pilgrimages, wars, and the frequent miseries of the nation. He covertly laid down the principles of this secret doctrine in the first four books of the Pentateuch, but withheld them from Deuteronomy. This constitutes the former the man, and the latter the woman. Moses also initiated the seventy elders into the secrets of this doctrine, and they again transmitted them from hand to hand. Of all who formed the unbroken line of tradition, David and Solomon were most initiated into the Kabbalah. No one, however, dared to write it down, till Simon ben Jochai, who lived at the time of the destruction of the second Temple . . .

After his death

His son, R. Eliezer, and his secretary, R. Abba, as well as his disciples, then collated R. Simon G. Jochai's treatises, and out of these composed the celebrated work called *Sohar* (r hz) i.e. *Splendour*, which is the grand storehouse of Kabbalism.[10]

Turning from tradition to history: though here again evidence is none too secure, the *Zohar* is attributed to Moses de Leon, a Qabalistic writer of the thirteenth century, and quite possibly parts of it were written by him. The whole compilation covers a vast ground and comprises:

1.   *The Sefer Ha-Zohar*, The Book of Splendour[11] - the main commentary.

2.   *The Sifra-di-Tseniuta*, The Book of the Veiled Mystery.[12] 3.   *The Sitré Torah*, Secrets of the Torah.

4.   *The Ra'ya Mahemna*, The True Shepherd.

5.   *The Midrush Ha-he'lam*, The Recondite Exposition.

6.   *The Tosefta*, Additions.

7.   *The Hekaloth*, Halls or Palaces.

8.   *The Idra Rabba*, The Greater Synod.[13]

9.   *The Idra Zuta*, The Lesser Synod.[14]

The first printed editions of the *Zohar* appeared almost simultaneously at Mantua and Cremona in 1558 - 60. Later editions are those of Lublin, 1623; Amsterdam, 1714 and 1805; Constantinople, 1736; and Venice. Of translations, Knorr von Rosenroth produced his *Kabbalah Denudata* in 1677-8, a Latin version of the *Sifra-di-Tseniuta*, the *Idra Rabba*, and *Idra Zuta*, which in 1887 were translated into English by S. L. Macgregor Mathers under the title of *The Kabbalah Unveiled*. In 1906, a complete translation of the *Zohar* into French was made by M. Jean de Pauly. Besides these, there is also the Soncino edition of the *Sefer Ha-Zohar;* this appeared in English between 1931 and 1934.

Of books dealing with the Qabalah there is a large number, of which the following is a small selection which may be useful to the student. *Qabbalah, The Philosophical Writings of Solomon Ben Yehudah Ibn Gebirol or Avicebron,* Isaac Myer, 1888; *La Kabbale ou La Philosophie Religieuse des Hébreux,* Ad. Franck, 1889. *The Kabbalah, Its Doctrines, Development, and Literature,* Christian D. Ginsburg, second impression, 1920. *The Holy Kabbalah,* A. E. Waite, 1929. *The Secret Doctrine of Israel,* A. E. Waite, 1913. *The History of Magic,* Eliphas Lévi, 1913. *The Book of Formation or Sepher Yetzirah,* Knut Stenring, 1923. *The Zohar in Moslem and Christian Spain,* Ariel Bension, 1932. *A Garden of Pomegranates,* Israel Regardie, 1932. *Q.B.L. or The Bride's Reception,* Frater Achad, 1922. *The Anatomy of the Body of God,* Frater Achad, 1925.

CHAPTER I

THE WISDOM OF THE QABALAH

The Qabalah

The Qabalah is not a holy book as are the *Vedas*, the *Bible*, and the *Koran*. It is not a book at all: instead it is a secret traditional knowledge, the hidden thought of Israel, which, like gold embedded in rock, is to be found only after much labour in many Hebrew works, such as the *Torah*, the *Talmud*, the

Mishna, Midrashim, Zohar, and scores of other books, the bewildering nature of which may be recognized in a few minutes by glancing through *A Talmudic Miscellany* by Paul Isaac Hershon.

The word hl bq (QBLH) is spelt in many ways, such as Qabalah, Qaballah, Cabala, Kaballa, and even, though quite incorrectly - Gabella. It is not derived from such fantastic origins as the name of Kapila, the Indian philosopher, or from the name of the goddess Cybele, for the word simply means "reception", something received an oral transmission, an oracle, or the spoken word. And the reason is, as we have already mentioned, that for ages the Qabalistic doctrines were not set down in writing or print, the Hebrews considering them too secret and sublime a wisdom for the common eye.

This wisdom is formed within a vast number of doctrines, such as the nature of God; the mystical cosmogony of the universe; the destiny of the universe; the creation of man; the immutability of God; the moral government of the universe; the doctrine of good and evil; the nature of the soul, angels, and demons; the transcendental symbolism of numbers and letters; the balancing of complementary forces, etc., etc. All these many problems are divided under two main headings, the Theoretical and the Practical Qabalah; the first being again divided into the Symbolical, Dogmatic, and Speculative branches. The first main division, that is the Theoretical, is philosophical; the second is magical and is largely elaborated round the Maaseh Merkabah - the Chariot of Ezekiel and the four Animals which are also mentioned in the *Apocalypse.* Out of this magical Qabalah much of the magic of the Middle Ages was developed.

The Speculative, or Metaphysical, Qabalah is the more important branch. It forms, as Adolph Franck says: "the heart and life of Judaism".[1] It covers the evolution, involution, and devolution of the universe in every conceivable spiritual, moral, and intellectual form; and under such symbolism as "The spirit clothes itself to come down and unclothes itself to go up"; and again in *Ecclesiastes,* "Who knoweth the spirit of man that goeth upward, and the spirit of the beast that goeth downward to the earth ?"[2]

All these doctrines are wrapped up in the most complete secrecy. They form, in fact, the ancient *Sod;* or Mystery, of the Hebrews.

Woe to the man who sees in the *Thorah,* i.e. Law, only simple recitals and ordinary words! Because, if in truth it only contained these, we would even today be able to compose a *Thorah* much more worthy of admiration. . . . The recitals of the *Thorah* are the vestments of the *Thorah.* Woe to him who takes this garment for the *Thorah* itself! . . . There are some foolish people who, seeing a man covered with a beautiful garment, carry their regard no further, and take the garment for the body, whilst there exists a still more precious thing, which is the soul. . . . The Wise, the servitors of the Supreme King, those who inhabit the heights of Sinai,[3] are occupied only with the soul, which is the basis of all the rest, which is the *Thorah* itself; and in the future time they will be prepared to contemplate the Soul of that Soul [i.e. the Deity] which breathes in the *Thorah.*[4]

This idea is again set forth in the *Zohar* in the following allegory:

Like unto a beautiful woman hidden in the interior of a palace who, when her friend and beloved passes by, opens for a moment a secret window, and is only seen by him; then again retires and disappears for a long time; so the doctrine shows herself only to the elect, but also not even to these always in the same manner. In the beginning, deeply veiled, she only beckons to the one passing, with her hand; it simply depends [on himself] if in his understanding he perceives this gentle hint. Later she approaches him somewhat nearer, and whispers to him a few words, but her countenance is still hidden in the thick veil, which his glances cannot penetrate. Still later she converses with him, her countenance covered with a thinner veil. After he has accustomed himself to her society, she finally shows herself to him face to face, and entrusts him with the innermost secrets of her heart [*Sod*].[5]

"It is", according to the *Book of Proverbs,*[6] "the glory of God to conceal a thing" - *Gloria Dei est Celare Verbum.* "With the lowly is wisdom"[7]; that is, wisdom belongs to those who have conquered the arrogance of the rational faculty. Moses is looked upon as such a one. He kept the secret law secretly and orally transmitted it to the elect;[8] also he compiled the public, or exoteric, law for the multitudes.

These two categories of laws are distinct, but frequently the second envelops the first, and, as pointed out in the Introduction, the uncovering of mysteries before the uninitiated is wrought with infernal dangers; for to do so wantonly is to blaspheme against the Mystery of God. As Éliphas Lévi writes:

Woe to those who lay bare the secret of divine generation to the impure gaze of the crowd. Keep the sanctuary shut, all ye who would spare your sleeping father the mockery of the imitators of Ham.[9] . . . The veil of Isis is not lifted with impunity, and curiosity blasphemes faith when Divine things are concerned. "Blessed are those who have not seen and have believed", says the Great Master. [10]

The Origins of the Qabala

The origins of the Qabalah are primeval; they are lost in the mists of legend, magic, and folklore. They have grown through a process of mystical integration until they have absorbed all the great myths of the world. The Qabalah is consequently a universal philosophy, combining the eternal masculine and the eternal feminine, and cementing them into the eternally human. So it happens that wherever we search we find origins. Thus in Essenism we find Qabalism. The Essenes were

not to divulge the secret doctrines to anyone . . . . carefully to preserve the books belonging to their sect and the names of the angels or the mysteries connected with the Tetragrammaton and the other names of God and the angels, comprised in the theosophy as well as with the cosmogony which also played so important a part among the Jewish mystics and the Kabbalists. [11]

But long before the Essenes existed lived the Qabalah. Aryan and Chaldean esoteric doctrines percolated into it. In Egypt, the mysteries of the Sun god, the Moon goddess, of Osiris and Isis, impinged upon it. Assyria and Babylon gave it much, and not a little may be traced to the *Vedas,* the *Upanishads,* the *Bhagavad-Gita,* and the *Vedantas,* and much of the Practical Qabalah to the *Tantras* more especially.

Historically, the main point of interest is that the Qabalist is an inveterate plagiarist; he never hesitates to absorb knowledge from outside. His doctrines, being secret, are vastly attractive; they suck in all mysteries and digest them into a universal form. Consequently there is both grist and chaff in the Qabalah, a medley of wisdom and nonsense which often defies separation. The outstanding advantage of this plagiarizing is that it offers something to everyone; consequently the Qabalah has developed into a world-embracing philosophy well adapted to the ideals of a world-scattered race. In it will be found Hinduism, Taoism, Buddhism, Zoroastrianism, Christianity, Theism, Deism, Dualism, Agnosticism, Pantheism, Satanism, Spiritualism, and Atheism; for every cult, except Polytheism, has burnt offerings on the altar of the Qabalistic mystery - magically depicted in the form of the Pan-like Baphomet.

It is this extraordinary universality which it is important to remember, for it has been the binding force which has kept Judaism intact; it has waterproofed it against solvent influences. Further still, the Qabalah does offer to humanity a world religion or cult. In a silent and secret way its doctrine is the conquering mystery of the life-force.

The Philosophy of the Qabalah

The philosophy of the Qabalah is not difficult to define; it is a question of balance, of poise, and of equilibrium. But to explain what is meant by balance or poise is not so easy, and in place of attempting to do so in a few sentences we will let this central principle evolve slowly on its own in this and the next four chapters.

Esoterically, the object of this philosophy is a return of the universe into the structure of the first Adam; this mystery we will attempt to explain later on. Exoterically it is the return of Israel to the Garden of Eden - the megalomania of the all-conquering Jew. The relationship between these two objects is that the second constitutes the protective shell of the first. The second maintains the Jewish peoples intact, and this intactness enables Qabalistic wisdom to evolve. Outside this protective duty, the second has no relationship to the first, no more than the shell of an egg - lifeless substance - has a relationship to the yolk within it - living substance. That the Israelites will find the Promised Land in the conquest of the world is a lie, a lie which protects a sublime truth - the reabsorption of the world into the pure spirit of God.

To the masses of the Jewish peoples such a statement will be considered blasphemous. Yet in the *Zohar* we read:

> With his ordinary understanding, man cannot understand the revelation of mysteries. All that I am about to reveal to you can be revealed only to the Masters, who know how to keep the balance because they have been initiated. [12]

The shell, the white, and the yolk form the perfect egg. The shell protects the white and the yolk, and the yolk feeds upon the white; and when the white has vanished, the yolk, in the form of the fledged bird, breaks through the shell and presently soars into the air. Thus does the static become the dynamic, the material the spiritual.

If the shell is the exoteric principle and the yolk the esoteric, what then is the white? The white is the food of the second, the accumulated wisdom of the world centering round the mystery of growth, which each single individual must absorb before he can break the shell. The transmutation of the white, by the yolk, into the fledgling is the secret of secrets of the entire Qabalistic philosophy.

"Know that all the upper and the lower worlds are comprised in the Image of God", we read in the *Zohar.*[13] Here we have: (1) a unity - the Image of God; (2) a duality - the Upper and Lower Worlds; (3) a trinity - the Upper and Lower Worlds and the Image of God; and (4) a quadruplicity - the Knower, the Upper World, the Lower World, and the Image of God. Yet this quadruplicity is in itself a duality - the Knower and the Image of God; because this Image includes the Upper and Lower Worlds. The absorption of the Knower in the Image is the Great Work - the re-establishment of unity or equilibrium.

Concerning the first of these two dualities, Isaac Myer writes:

The basic element of most of the ancient, and to this day, of many of the modern religions of the world is, the *idea* of a perfect invisible universe above, which is the real and true paradigm or ideal model, of the visible universe below, the latter being the reflection, a simulacrum or shadow, of the invisible perfect ideal above. This idea was fully understood by the Ancient Egyptians, as was shown in their deities Nut or Neith, the Upper World, Shu or Mâ, the Intermediary, and Seb, the Earth.[14] In India, the same idea is fully set forth in the esoteric books of the *Vedas,* called the *Upanishads.* It is the supreme Ideal Brahm which is the only True. It manifests Itself first in Brama, Vishnu and Siva, past, present and future time, and through these in the visible, the last being Maya, or Illusion. The temples of most of the archaic peoples of Asia and of Egypt were intended to be visible copies of the heavenly Temple, the starry firmament called *Templum,* and the same idea is visible in those of the Hebrews. Philo and Josephus represent the Temples of the Israelites, as typical of the visible universe, and this was based on the invisible universe. [15]

Amongst the Mohammedans we find the same idea: the first thing God created was a pen.

Indeed the whole creation is but a Transcript, and God when He made the World, did but write it out of that Copy which He had of it in His Divine understanding from all Eternity. The Lesser Worlds (Mikrokosmos) or Men, are but transcripts of the Greater (the Makrokosmos), as Children and Books are the copies of themselves. 16

God takes upon himself spiritual form in the act of creation, which is pure light transfigured into visible light, which is the relationship between the eyes and pure light. Pure spirit can only be sensed as a relation which we call spirituality - the relationship between the third eye and pure spirit. God to this third eye is not Nothing, he is All Things; for when this eye is open he can be seen everywhere. The idea *ex nihilo nihil fil*[17] (from nothing nothing is made) is abhorrent to the Qabalah.

Not any Thing [says the *Zohar*] is lost in the universe, not even the vapour which goes out of our mouths; as all things, it has its place and its destination, and the Holy One, blessed be It, makes it concur to Its works; not anything falls into the void, not even the words and the voice of man, but all has its place and its destination. [18]

The Qabalist Abram ben Dior writes:

Then they [the Qabalists] affirm, that All Things have been drawn from No-Thing [not Nothing], they do not wish to speak of nothing properly to say, for never can Being come from Non-being, but they understand, by Non-being, that which one can conceive of, neither by its cause or its essence; it [the No-Thing] is, in a word, the Cause of Causes; it is It whom we call the Primordial Non-being, because it is anterior to the entire universe. [19]

Though the Qabalah recognizes but one primordial cause, it also recognizes two complementary elements: the one incorruptible and vital which reveals itself as a spiritual energy, and the other corruptible and inert, always tending to dissolve and return to its original atoms. The first is Bliss, the second is Hate: the first is symbolized by the angelic hosts, the second by the demon hordes - Good and Evil; for, as Isaiah says: "I form the light, and create darkness: I make peace, and create evil :I the Lord do all these things." [20]

The spirit which we sense through our third eye is not God as the Primordial Cause, or No-Thing, but as it were the Thought of this Cause. "He constituted in the first place a point of light, which became the Divine Thought." [21] Our consciousness is the mirror which catches the rays of this Thought; therefore all thoughts are images of God's Thought, and the more spiritual, alive, our consciousness becomes, the more perfect are these images, which are not illusions but symbols of Reality.

Simon ben Yohai stretched out his hands and cried:

Now ponder well upon all that I have this day revealed unto you! And know that none of these celestial palaces are light, nor are they spirits, nor are they souls, nor are they any form that may be seized hold of by any of the senses. Know that the Palaces are *Thoughts-seen through curtains*. Take away the thought, and the Palace becomes nothing that the mind can grasp nor the imagination picture! And know, finally, that all the mysteries of the Faith lie in this doctrine: that all that exists in the Upper World is the *Light of Thought- The infinite.* Lift the curtain, and all matter appears immaterial! Lift another curtain, and the immaterial becomes even more spiritual and sublime! As each succeeding curtain is lifted we are transported to ever-higher planes of sublimity until the *Highest* is reached![22]

The curtains are the divisions (abysses) between the superconscious Thought of God and the conscious thought of man. The ultimate curtain is the shell of the egg - materiality; but before this final curtain can be lifted, a host of intellectual curtains - the white of the egg - have to be dissolved by transmutation into spiritual energy. Spiritual deliverance, or attainment, is consequently an act of creation.

Finally we come to this conclusion: It is not God, or the Universe, which is the supreme mystery, but man, man himself, the link between God and the Universe. The *Zohar* says:

As soon as man appeared, all was achieved, both in the upper and in the lower worlds. For all is contained in man. He combines within himself all the forms.[23]

Again the *Zohar* says

The Essence of the Supreme Wisdom is composed of earth and of heaven; of divine and of human; of material and of immaterial, even as man is composed of body and soul. Man is the synthesis of all the Holy Names. In man are enclosed all the worlds, both the upper and the lower. Man includes all the mysteries, even those that existed before the creation of the world.

Since the form of man comprises all that is in the heavens above and on the earth beneath, God has chosen it as *His Own Form*. Naught could exist before the formation of the human form which encloses all things. And all that exists is by the grace of the existence of the human form. But we must distinguish between the upper man and the lower man, since one cannot exist without the other. On the form of man depends the perfection of faith. That which we call heavenly man, or the first divine manifestation, is the absolute form of all that is, the source of all forms and ideas: *Supreme Thought*. Man is the central point around which all creation revolves. He is the noblest figure of all those that are harnessed to the Chariot of God. [24]

In Nature, man is the centre and the world is the periphery of what the *Zohar* calls the garment of God, [25] and the removal of this garment mysteriously does not disclose what lies behind it, but what lies within ourselves. It is not that we are absorbed by God, but that God is absorbed by us - the ocean of quicksilver merging into the minutest globule of this same metal. This unclothing is accomplished through equilibrium, not of opposite, but of complementary forces. Evil is not the opposite of good, but the negative side of a positive-negative existence called life. When the positive equals, or balances, the negative, the result is equilibrium. Perfect equilibrium is Zero, that is No-thing - Bliss.

Equilibrium

Equilibrium is the fundamental law, or mystery, of the Qabalah; in fact the bulk of the Qabalistic doctrines are but a commentary upon it. There is the Upper and the Lower, the Real and the Apparent, the Invisible and the Visible. In the *Zohar* we read:

All that which is found [or exists] upon the Earth has its spiritual counterpart also to be found on High, and there does not exist the smallest thing in the world which is not itself attached to something on High, and is not found in dependence upon it. When the inferior part is influenced, and that which is set over it in the Superior world is equally [influenced], all are perfectly united together. [26]

Again and again is this idea repeated in different words, and from it is derived the Talmudic maxim, "If thou wilt know the invisible, have an open eye for the visible", which means that this world is the true Bible which can lead us back to God or Reality; "for all which is contained in the Lower World is also found in the Upper [in prototype]. The Lower and Upper reciprocally act upon each other." [27] Or as is written in the *Sepher Shephathal*:

All that which is on the earth is also found above [in perfect prototype], and there is not anything so insignificant in the world that does not depend upon another above: in such a manner, that if the lower moves itself the higher corresponding to it moves towards it. As to the number, therefore, of the different species of creatures, which are enumerated below, the same number is to be found in the upper roots. [28]

This doctrine of interdependence runs through the *New Testament*. Christ says:

Take heed that ye despise not one of these little ones; for I say unto you, That in heaven their angels do always behold the face of my Father which is in heaven. [29]

Also:

Are not two sparrows sold for a farthing? and one of them shall not fall on the ground without your Father. [30]

"Who?" *(Mee)* and "What?" *(Maah)* are the two extremes of this doctrine, representing as they do the "Above" and the "Below". In "Who" created "these" is to be found the origin of the word *Elohim,* that is God (Gods) for in Hebrew "these" is *Eleh* (hl a) and by adding *Mee* (ym) we obtain *Elohim* (myhla) the *Mee* being reversed on account of its reflection. "And upon this secret the world is built." [31]

This same idea of equilibrium between Who and What - Upper and Lower - is also found in the Hermetic doctrines, which drew largely on Qabalistic knowledge. All is expressed in one proposition:

"That which is above is like that which is below, and that which is below is like that which is above, for the fulfilment of the wonders of the one thing." According to Éliphas Lévi this universal principle is "the TELESMA of the world".[32] To symbolize this supreme truth, Hermes, so legend affirms, duplicated the serpent on his caduceus and so set it against itself in eternal equilibrium. (See Plate I on page 18 and 19.)

In the visible world, man is the centre, just as God is the centre of the invisible world.

God created man in His Own Image. . . . Adam was made of the same earth out of which was raised the *Sanctuary of the Earth.* And the earth on which was the sanctuary was the synthesis of the four cardinal points of the world. These cardinal points were united at the moment of creation with the four elements fire, water, air, and earth . .[33]

these elements being ∞*od, Heh, Vau,* and *Heh* of the name Jehovah. Man is consequently the synthesis of "all the Holy Names",[34] therefore in man are "enclosed all the worlds, both the upper and the lower", and:

Since the form of man comprises all that is in the heavens above and on the earth beneath, God has chosen it as *His Own Form.* Naught could exist before the formation of the human form which encloses all things. And all that exists is by the grace of the existence of the human form.[35] (See Diagram 1 on page 20.)

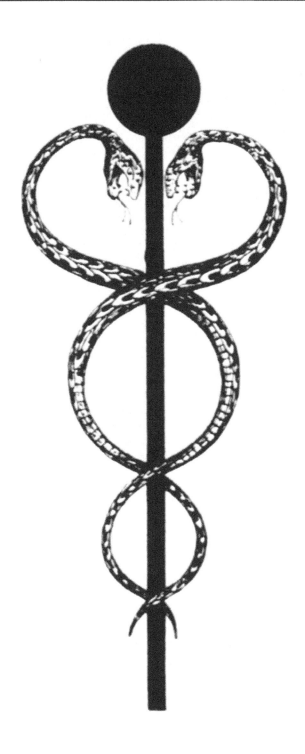

Plate 1: The Caduceus of Hermes

Plate 1: The Winged Wand of Egypt

Diagram 1: The Divine Man As man is a duality in unity, so also is the Garden of Eden. There is the Heavenly Eden to which there is no human approach, and the Earthly Eden which is approached by thirty-two paths - the 22 letters and 10 numerals.

No one knows the Earthly Eden but the Little Face [the seven lower Sephiroth], and no one knows the Heavenly Eden but the Great Face [the three Supernal Sephiroth]. . . . Should the Upper Eye [Kether] cease looking into the Lower Eye [Malkuth], the world would perish. [36]

Thus does this unvarying idea of balance run on.

"The union of man with God", says Saint Theresa, "is nothing but the reunion of two bodies which have been separated but are always one." The connecting link is the power of will, which is neither good nor evil, but a power or energy, which can be filtered through good or evil. It is, as it were, the beam of light of a magic lantern, the slides it penetrates being the nature of man. As long as these slides exist there can be no perfect vision of God and, consequently, no perfect union. When Moses said to God, "I beseech Thee, show me Thy glory", the answer he received was:

Thou canst not see my face: for there shall no man see me, and live. And the Lord said, Behold, there is a place by me, and thou shalt stand upon a rock: And it shall come to pass, while my glory passeth by, that I will put thee in a clift of the rock, and will cover thee with my hand while I pass by: And I will take away mine hand, and thou shalt see my back parts: but my face shall not be seen. [37]

Which means that man, if he wills, can see God's lower manifestation - his visible universe - but that his invisible nature is cut off from him whilst in the flesh.

Since this fundamental law of equilibrium was first grasped, and it sinks back long before Qabalistic days, nothing has been added to the essential knowledge of man; and the philosophy of the Classical Age, the magic of the Medieval, and the science of the Modern Ages are founded upon it and have, in attempting to explain it, merely replaced one set of symbols by another. The *Zohar* says:

The Holy One, blessed be He, found it necessary to create all these things in the world to ensure its permanence, so that there should be, as it were, a brain with many membranes encircling it. The whole world is constructed on this principle, upper and lower, from the first mystic point up to the furthest removed of all the stages. They are all coverings one to another, brain within brain and spirit within spirit, so that one is a shell to another. The primal point is the innermost light of a translucency, tenuity, and purity, passing comprehension. [38]

Philosophical comparisons

Before concluding this chapter, it may be of some interest to the reader if a few brief comparisons are made between the Qabalistic doctrines and other philosophies, because this will accentuate its universality; for the Qabalah is a world philosophy, and consequently there lurks within it the makings of a world religion. That it should show remarkable resemblance's to Zoroastrianism is to be expected, for both flourished in adjacent regions. As the Qabalah is largely an exposition of the Upper and Lower, God and the Image of God, so is the Zoroastrian philosophy founded on the idea of the passive and active in Nature - the so-called good and the evil. As to the Qabalist the mediating agent is the will, so to the Zoroastrian the Great Magical Agent is in actual fact no other than Lucifer - the vehicle of light.

To Pythagoras, God was absolute truth clothed in light, all things emerged from the tetrad, and the mediator was number manifested by form. To him material forms were but images or illusions of real forms, and this was the view also taken by Aristotle and Plato. To the second of these philosophers "God, intending to make a visible world, first formed an intelligible one; that so having an incorporeal and most god-like pattern before Him, He might make the corporeal world agreeable to it". Xenophon says: "The Supreme God holds himself invisible, and it is only in his works that we are capable of admiring him." [39]

And Cicero says, "Though you see not the Deity, yet by the contemplation of his works, you are led to acknowledge a God".[40] which is similar to St. Paul when, speaking of Christ, he said: "For the invisible things of him from the creation of the world are clearly seen, being understood by the things that are made, even his eternal power and Godhead." [41] And again: "For in him we live, and move, and have our being; as certain also of your own poets have said, For we are also his offspring." [42]

But of all philosophies the closest-allied are those of the Vedanta and of Lao-Tze. The Indian system is a trinity in unity, the ineffable, incomprehensible Brahm becoming apparent in the Trimurti *(tri =* three and *murti* = bodies), Brama, Vishnu, and Siva - creation, preservation, and destruction. The Âtman is Reality, and the apparent world is Mâyâ, or illusion. Man within him possesses an âtman, or soul, which can only attain to Reality through absorption by the Âtman or over-soul. This absorption is effected through meditation.

Taoism is in idea even more closely related. "Tao produced one, one produced two, two produced three, and three produced all things." What, then, is Tao?

There was a time when Heaven and Earth did not exist, but only an unlimited Space in which reigned absolute immobility. All the visible things and all that which possesses existence were born in that Space from a powerful principle, which existed by Itself, and from Itself developed Itself, and which made the heavens revolve and preserved the universal life; a principle as to which philosophy declares we know not the name, and which, for that reason, it designates by the simple appellation Tao. . . . Tao manifested itself in Heaven and Earth, with which it is, so to say, One. [43]

Another writer says

By the Chinese, man is considered as a mikrokosm, the universe is man on a large scale. . . . Human reason is the reason of the universe The holy-man, or sage by eminence, is like the great pinnacle and spirit. He is the first of all beings. His spirit is one with the heavens, the master work of the Supreme Reason, being perfectly unique. [44]

These resemblances - and scores of others could be cited - are not fortuitous, neither is it possible that they should have originated from one source, one human philosophical doctrine. The truth is that they are spontaneous, they spring naturally from reason itself once thought is turned upon the world; they are an integral part of man's mind and being. Destroy them, and we are plunged into madness; fertilize them, and step by step we are raised towards God. Religion, that is the equilibrium between the visible and the invisible, the lower and the upper, is essentially a part of man's nature. When this equilibrium is lost, society, however progressive it may seem materially, is plunged back into chaos from which cosmos and order can only emerge by an illumination, a balancing of forces, which will give life and light to a new world order. Man is the Microcosm, because he cannot truly and meaningly say "I am" without postulating the Macrocosm. The one is as much of his nature as the other, because his existence depends on the balance between both as certainly as an electrical current depends on what we call positive and negative waves of electricity or of light. "Let there be Light" occultly represents the world, not only as a material form, but as a spiritual idea.

CHAPTER II

THE COSMOGONY OF THE QABALAH

The Primal Cause.

In its most condensed form the cosmogony of the Qabalah may be defined as a process of world emanation from No-Thing, through the form of man, back again to No-Thing; man being the equilibrating centre. In idea it is little removed from the latest conception of science, which looks upon the universe as something which has "condensed" out of the immaterial into the material, and which in the course of time will be radiated back into immateriality. Further, that the material is only cognizable through the mind of man.

The Primal Cause is called the Ayin (Oya) - the No-Thing; that is a Something which, transcending the human intellect, can only be described negatively.

It is so named because we do not know, and it is impossible to know, that which there is in this Principle, because it never descends as far as our ignorance and because it is above Wisdom itself.[1]

Out of this No-Thing emerges as it were the Ain Soph, the Endlessness, Boundlessness, and Eternality of No-Thing - therefore, in a way, a qualified No-Thingness. In the *Book of Job* we read: "He stretcheth out the north over the empty place, and hangeth the earth upon nothing."[2] It is also called Attikah D'Attikin, the Ancient of all the Ancients, and Attikah Qadosha, the Sacred Ancient; it is sexless and is sometimes described as the Non-Ego or Not-I, the Ayin being altogether beyond the I.

In the *Zohar* we read

And there went forth, as a sealed secret, from the head of Ain Soph, a nebulous spark of matter without shape or form, a centre of a circle, neither white nor black, neither red nor green, in fact without any colour.[3]

This is the Ain Soph Aur - Light, not as a contradistinction to Darkness, but as a vibration. First, so the symbolism describes, the Ain Soph withdrew Itself into Itself to form an infinite space - the Abyss. In this space appeared a point of light, or life-giving energy, which filled it. The Ain Soph Aur is, consequently, pictured as contraction and expansion, a sucking-in and throwing-out within itself; it therefore symbolizes the centripetal and centrifugal energies of creation, which through their rhythm constitute the Infinite Light out of which the universe is made; this Light has been called the Idealized Blood of the Universe.

This trinity of Primal Causes - the Ayin, the Ain Soph, and the Ain Soph Aur - is concealed in the first three verses of the *Book of Genesis*: the creation out of God, since everything in "the heavens and the earth" comes from the No-Thing; the Spirit of God; and the Light which emanated from God's Spiritual Voice (the totality of the 22 letters) or words - "Let there be Light". The graspable beginning is Light; all before it or, so to say, behind or beyond it, is impenetrable mystery - an Absolute Darkness to the mind.

From the Ain Soph Aur emanates Ehyeh (hyha), the"I" or "I Am" - abstract thought; then YHVH (hvhy),"It who was, and is, and will be" - thought in time; and lastly Elohim (myhla),God in nature and God in the *Bible,* in which YHVH (Jehovah or Yahweh) is translated as "Lord", the equivalent of the Hebrew Adonai, for the true name of Tetragrammaton (YHVH) may not be pronounced.

Thus, as the Ayin, Ain Soph, and Ain Sopb Aur form a group of three unthinkable principles, so do Ehyeh, YHVH, and Elohim form a group of three intelligent principles - abstract thoughts, thought in time and thought in everything; for the whole universe arose out of the Voice (the creative instrument) which expressed the ineffable thought of Light in the words "*Yehe Aur*" - "Let there be Light". Thus to the Qabalist the universe is a divine form reflected in a beam of light, a form which will vanish utterly back into the Ayin when this beam is cut off. Existence, therefore, is Light; perhaps that light which present-day science calls "radiation".

The Sephirotic Scheme

According to the *Zohar* the act of creation took place as follows:

When the most Mysterious wished to reveal Himself, He first produced a single point which was transmuted into a thought, and in this He executed innumerahle designs, and engraved innumerable gravings. He further graved within the sacred and mystic lamp a mystic and most holy design, which was a wonderous edifice issuing from the midst of thought. [4]

This edifice is Elohim, the conjunction of the "Who" and the "These", as already explained. Again we read:

Before God created the world, His name was enclosed within Him, and therefore He and His name enclosed within Him were not one. Nor could this unity be effected until He created the world. Having, therefore, decided to do so, He traced and built, but the aim was not attained until He enfolded Himself in a covering of a supernal radiance of thought and created therefrom a world. He produced from the light of that supernal radiance mighty cedars [six days of creation] of the Upper World, and placed His chariot on twenty-two graven letters which were carved in ten utterances [the numerals or Sephiroth] and infixed there. [5]

As long as God's name was enclosed within Him, No-Thingness persisted; for unity can only become perceptible through a difference. This difference was thought, out of which the world was created. Thoughts are expressed in words formed from the alphabet of 22 letters and the numerals 0 to 9.

In thirty-two mysterious paths of Wisdom did the Lord write. . . He created His Universe by the three forms of expression: Numbers, Letters, and Words. Ten ineffable Sephiroth and twenty-two basal letters: three mothers [a (A), *Aleph,* air; m (M), *Mem,* water; W (Sh), *Shin,* fire], seven double [B G D K P R Th], and twelve simple [letters] [H V Z Ch T I L N S O Tz Q.] [6]

The "single point which was transmuted into a thought" is the first Sephirah,[7] Kether or Crown. "It is the Principle of all the Principles, the Mysterious Wisdom, the Crown of all that which there is of the Most High, the Diadem of the Diadems."[8] The divine name in Kether is Ehyeh, "I am.

The Sephirotic Scheme (see Plate II on page 25) may be condensed as follows: Kether is also called Abbah, the Father; it is the Will or Ego from which the remaining nine Sephiroth emanate. The second Sephirah is Binah, the Universal Intellect or Understanding, also called Immah or Mother. Whilst Kether is positive, form (male), Binah is negative and plastic, the receiver of form and, therefore, matter (female), because "Everything existing can only be the work of the male and female" principles. [9]

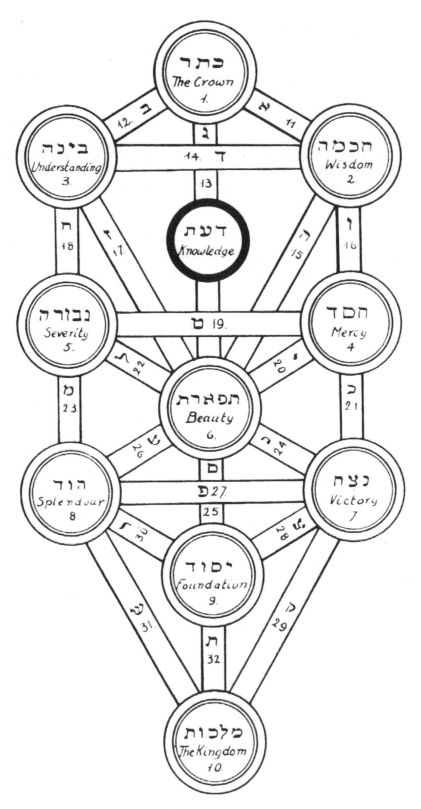

Plate 2: The Tree of Life The second emanation from Kether is called 'Hokmah, Wisdom, the Word, Logos, or Son; it is the male principle in activity, for through it all things are generated. "By means of the thirty-two paths . . . it gives everything, existing, shape and size." [10] This Sephirah is the

Spiritus Mundi. From 'Hokmah is derived the balance of the Sephiroth, the next six of which refer to the dimensions of the universe - length, breadth, and depth moving as it were outwardly towards the positive and the negative, the male and the female principles each, therefore, in two directions. Together they form the six faces of a perfect cube (the Stone of the Wise): the tenth Sephirah, Malkuth, the Kingdom or Sabbath represents rest, poise, and completion.

These first three Sephiroth - Kether, Binah, and 'Hokmah (Father, Mother, and Son) - the Supernal Triad - constitute the Intelligible or Intellectual World.

And since the Holy Ancient is expressed and impressed by three [i.e. Ayin, Ain Soph, and Ain Soph Aur the expression; and Kether, Binah, 'Hokmah the impression], so also all the lamps that receive their light from the Holy Ancient are triadic. [11]

The second triad is called the Moral or Sensuous World; it is the World Soul which emanates from the World Spirit *(Spiritus Mundi).* It consists of the positive or male principle 'Hesed, which means Grace or Mercy, also called Gedulah (Magnificence); and the negative or female principle Pahad (Punishment), also called Geburah (Severity) and Din (Judgment). These two unite in the sixth Sephirah, Tiphereth (Beauty), the highest manifestation of ethical life - the Ideal.

The third triad is called the Physical or Material World and consists of the male or positive Sephirah Netzah (Triumph or Victory), and the female or negative Hod (Glory or Splendour). They constitute the "arms of God" and represent the centripetal and centrifugal energies of the universe, for "All the energies, forces, and increase in the universe proceed through them".[12] In turn they unite in the Sephirah Yesod (Foundation), the principle of all generation. They represent the Deity "as the universal power, creator, and generator of all the existences".

As this third triad is the *natura naturans,* so is the tenth and last Sephirah the *natura naturata* - the material world, namely Malkuth, tbe Kingdom.

This Sephirah represents the feet of the Heavenly Adam (about whom more anon), his head resting in Kether, and in it the name of the Deity is Adonai, the Lord - that is the ineffable YHVH. Malkuth is also called the queen, the Matrona, the Matron, the Daughter, Bride, the Shekinah (the Real Presence of the Deity), and Harmony.

Finally we obtain a fourth triad, a synthetic one formed out of Kether, Tiphereth, and Malkuth. The first influences the Neshamah, the spirit and moral consciousness; the second influences the Rua'h, the reason and intellectual faculty; and the third the Nephesh, the instincts, sentiments, and emotions, the animal life in man.

Thus from the Ain Soph Aur flow out the ten Sephiroth or Principles; hence the decade is considered the perfect number by the Qabalah, the all-embracing unit emerging from the No-Thing (0 - 1), and the unity which ultimately is to be radiated back into NoThingness (1 - 0)

Origin of the Sephiroth

Before we examine each Sephirah in turn, it may be of some interest to the reader to enquire into the origins of this philosophical system. Though pre-eminently Jewish, it is nevertheless eminently universal. The word is probably derived from r ps *Sapheir,* which means "to number" or "to count", and the ten Sephiroth are frequently abbreviated as s "y and *Samekh* + ∞*od* equal 70, the numerical value of dvs *Sod,* Secret; they are consequently occult numbers.

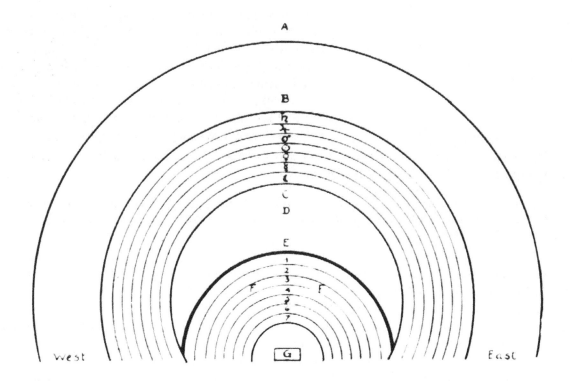

This diagram represents a half-section, divided perpendicularly, of the inverted bowlshaped universe. AB, BC, CE, and EG are the four worlds. AB is the Father, Anu or Kether; BC the Sun, Bel or 'Hokmah; CE the Mother, Ea or Binah. Above all is Ao or El – the Ayin. a is the Zodiac, the Great Ocean called the Deep and the Abyss; B is the zone of the fixed stars; A to c is the upper firmament; and C to E the lower firmament. A to B is the zone of the spirits of heaven and B to c the zone of the planets. C to E is the zone of winds, storms, and clouds; E is the convex hollow earth shell; FF is the concave hollow underworld of seven zones; realm of the ghost world; and G is the Nadir or Root – in it are the Waters of Life and the Throne of Chaos and below it are 21 hells.

Plate 3: The Chaldean and Hebrew Cosmos

Isaac Myer finds a remarkable similarity between the cosmos of the *Zohar* and that of the ancient Chaldeans. He writes:

In AB, BC, CE, and EG [see Plate III on page 27], we have similarities to the Four Worlds. The three great heavens answer to the Upper Three Sephiroth. I. That of the Father Abbah, or *Kether,* the

Crown, to *Anu,* afterwards *Ana;* the place of the aether or highest sublimated air or atmosphere. II. The Son, *Bel, El* or *Baal,* the sublimated fire, answering to *'Hokhmah,* Wisdom. III. The Mother, Immah, to *Ea,* the sublimated water, to *Binah,* the comprehending Intellect. Above all these is *Ao, Ilu* or *El,* the unknown ideal deity; which parallels the *Ain Soph,* Endless, to man's comprehension NoThing. This unknown ideal deity held the highest place in the Chaldean Mythology. Under these were the seven planets in their seven orbits, or spheres; the probable germ of the idea of the Sephiroth, or media between the Highest and Lowest worlds. [12]

Historically interesting as these general origins are, philosophically the most important correspondences are those connected with the Sephirah 'Hokmah; for in many places in the *Old Testament* and in the *New,* especially in the works of St. Paul and St. John, is Wisdom described as the creative power. The *Book of Genesis* opens with the words "In the beginning", which in Hebrew are rendered by the word *B'raishith,* which by many Qabalists is spelt *Be'Raishith,* which means "through Wisdom", or through the Word or principle which expresses Wisdom - namely the Logos of Philo and St. John. A similar idea is found in the Chaldaic word Memrah, in the Vach of the *Rig Veda,* Honover of the *Zend Avesta,* and in the Boundless Light of latter-day Buddhists.

Nebo was the Babylonian god of Wisdom, and his planet was Mercury. Moses, the supposed originator of the Qabalah, was buried on Mount Nebo. Bo, Bod, Boden, and in China Fo, are all gods of Wisdom. Amongst the Buddhists and Brahmins the day of Wisdom is Wednesday. Amongst the Scandinavians we have Wo, Wod, and Woden; in Egypt, Thoth; in Classical Greece, Hermes; and among the Romans, Mercury - all gods of Wisdom, whose day is the fourth day of the week, Wednesday, upon which God created "lights in the firmament of the heaven to divide the day from the night". [13]

Wisdom is not only the creator of the Universe but also the Mediator between the Uncreated and the Created - God and Man. In the form of 'Hokmah, the son of Kether, Wisdom renders comprehensive the abstract thought in an association of ideas. Philo names it Messiah, and St. John Christ. St. Paul says:

But we speak the wisdom of God in a mystery, even the hidden wisdom, which God ordained before the world unto our glory: Which none of the princes of this world knew: for had they known it, they would not have crucified the Lord of glory. [14]

Referring to Christ as the Sun, this same Apostle says:

Who is the image of the invisible God, the firstborn of every creature: For by him were all things created, that are in heaven, and that are in earth, visible and invisible, whether they be thrones, or dominions, or principalities, or powers: all things were created by him, and for him: And he is before all things, and by him all things consist [exist ?]. [15]

Many other comparisons could be given, but the above must suffice to show how deep-rooted are the origins of the Sephirotic Scheme, and how surely they have branched upwards into the mystical foundations of Christianity.

The Ten Sephiroth

(1) r Uk Kether, the Crown. As we have explained, this first Sephirah represents "I am" as being, that is as pure existence. It is neither positive nor negative, but ±, and though sexless it is androgenous. Though the primordial point of light, it is nevertheless the circumference of all things, the centre of which is nowhere because it is in No-Thing; containing all the potency of Tetragrammaton (YHVH), it is simultaneously past, present, and future. In the letter ∞ *od,* which corresponds to it, is enclosed the imminence of the ten Sephiroth. Frequently it is called the Ancient of the Ancients, the Ancient, or the Ancient of Days. For instance, in the *Book of Daniel* we read:

I beheld till the thrones were cast down, and the Ancient of days did sit, whose garment was white as snow, and the hair of his head like the pure wool: his throne was like the fiery flame, and his wheels as burning fire. [16]

Kether is also called the White Head, the Long Face, Macroprosopos, and Adam Qadmon or Adam Illaah - the Supernal or Primordial or Heavenly Adam. The remaining Sephiroth are the Short Face.

In the angelic order, Kether is represented by the Beasts of Ezekiel, the Holy Living Creatures of the Chariot-Throne, namely the four Kerubim - the Eagle, Man, Lion, and Bull - which represent the four elements Air (Smell), Water (Taste), Fire (Sight), and Earth (Touch). Also it includes in its mysterious nature the four letters of Tetragrammaton as follows: y (Lion), h (Man), v (Eagle), and h (Bull). But as in itself Kether is also the Shekinah (the Glory of God), in it is hidden the *Shin* (w), which symbolizes Spirit.

As the Ain Soph is represented by the closed eye, so is Kether represented by the open eye. (Compare the eye of Shiva in Hindu mythology.) As long as this eye remains open the universe is maintained in being, but when it shuts it vanishes into Non-being, that is No-Thingness. In the threefold division of man's nature, Kether represents the Neshamah or spirit.

(2) r nyb Binah, Mind. This Sephirah is sometimes placed second and sometimes third, and it is generally called the Understanding. It is feminine and negative - the matter, as it were, in which Kether can take form and propagates itself. Binah is often called the Heavenly Mother or Holy Spirit. Her letter is h *(Heh),* the numerical value of which is 5. Binah possesses 50 gates, which is symbolical of the *Heh* multiplied by the ∞*od;* her symbol is the dove; her dimension is depth, whilst Kether's is length (compare the lingam and yoni in Hindu mythology); and her colour is sky blue, the colour of the Virgin Mary. From the union between Kether and Binah emanates 'Hokmah.

(3) hmk C 'Hokmah, Wisdom. The third Sephirah is the Son or Logos and the Firstborn. It represents abstract ideas, the fruit of the "I am" forming in the mind. In the Qabalah it is often called "The Only Begotten Son". "In the beginning was the Word, and the Word was with God, and the Word was God" [17] Here we have presented to us the Logos nature of 'Hokmah. Its colour is yellow or red-orange, the colour of Christ; it is positive and male, and its letter is v *(Vau* = 6), which multiplied by the 50 Gates of Binah reveals w *(Shin* = 300), the Glory of God. The final h *(Heh)* of Tetragrammaton represents the remaining seven Sephiroth.

This revelation of the *Shin* shows the triadic nature of the first three Sephiroth which constitute the Intellectual World, and it closely relates it to many mysteries. Thus, in ydw Shaddai (Almighty), the name of the Deity before he revealed himself as YHVH, the *Shin* comes first; in Messiah (hywm) and the exoteric Jesus (ovwy) it comes second; in the esoteric Yeheshuah (hvwhy) it comes in the middle; and in Serpent (whk) it comes last. In Yeheshuah it is the letter of Mercy, for it is the central equilibrating fire; in all the others it is the letter of wrath, for it is out of equilibrium, and particularly so in Shaddai and the Serpent.

In actual conception these three Sephiroth form a trinity in unity of knowledge, that which knows and that by which it is known; they unite in themselves everything and are themselves united to the No-Thing.

(4) ds c , 'Hesed, Grace, Love, Mercy, or Compassion. From 'Hokmah emanate six Sephiroth, which, as we have explained, symbolize the dimensions of matter. 'Hesed is the Right Arm of Macrocosmos; it endows the world with feeling and sentiment.

(5) dhp, Pahad, Rigour, Punishment, Fear, or Severity. This Sephirah is the Left Arm of Macrocosmos. It is feminine and passive, as 'Hesed is masculine and active. As 'Hesed symbolizes life, so does Pahad symbolize death.

(6) ur a pu Tiphereth, Beauty. This Sephirah is the common centre or harmony of 'Hesed and Pahad, of life and death, the active and passive in the Moral World. Its symbol is the Sun, the heart of the

universe and also the heart of Adam Qadmon - the Supernal Adam. Tiphereth is the seat of sentiment and the ethical qualities; it is inhabited by the Rua'h - the Reasoning Soul.

(7)   c x n Netzah, Triumph, Firmness, or Victory. This is the first of the three energetic principles. It represents the right leg and thigh of Macrocosmos.

(8)   dvh Hod, Splendour, or Glory. This is the left leg and thigh of Macrocosmos.

By Triumph and Glory, we comprehend extension, multiplication and force; because all the forces which were born into the universe went out of their bosom, and it is for this reason, that these two Sephiroth are called: the armies of YHVH. [18]

(9)   dvs y Yesod, Foundation. This Sephirah is the seat of the generative principle.

Everything shall return to its Foundation, from which it has proceeded. All marrow, seed and energy are gathered in this place. [19]

(10) uvk l m Malkuth, Kingdom, or Dominion. As Kether is the harmony at the beginning, so is Malkuth the harmony at the end; the first the head and the last the feet of Adam Qadmon. The divine name attached to this Sephirah is Adonai - the Tetragrammaton. Malkuth is also called the Queen, Shekinah, and Havah - Eve. It is the seat of the Nephesh, the instincts, and its angel is Metatron, the Angel of the Covenant, the letters of whose name equal in numerical value those of Shaddai, namely 314.

Behold, I send an Angel before thee, to keep thee in the way, and to bring thee into the place which I have prepared. Beware of him, and obey his voice, provoke him not: for he will not pardon your transgressions: for my name is in him. [20]

The Tree of Life.

The ten Sephiroth when combined with the twenty-two letters form what is known as the Tree of Life, which constitutes the framework of Adam Qadmon, the Heavenly Adam, similar in anatomy to his human counterpart - the Earthly Adam. Man is a combination of three spheres of force, the intellectual, the moral, and the physical, which are related to the Neshamah, Rua'h, and Nephesh. These forces, or qualities, find their activity in the outer or material world, which is alone cognizable and, therefore, existent to man because of his three-fold constitution.

Like the body of man, the Tree of Life is itself divided horizontally into four planes (see Plate IV on page 31) and vertically by three trunks or pillars (see Plate IV on page 32). The central pillar - known as Harmony, or Mildness, or sometimes as the Perfect Pillar, consisting of Kether, Tiphereth, Yesod, and Malkuth - is the Tree of Life as mentioned in the *Book of Genesis*. The right-hand pillar - that of 'Hokmah, 'Hesed, and Netza'h - is active, male, and positive, and is called the pillar of Mercy, whilst that of Binah, Pahad, and Hod is passive, female, and negative, and is called the pillar of Justice. These two pillars constitute the Tree of the Knowledge of Good and Evil, because they are made up of unbalanced forces which can only find equilibrium in the central trunk or pillar.

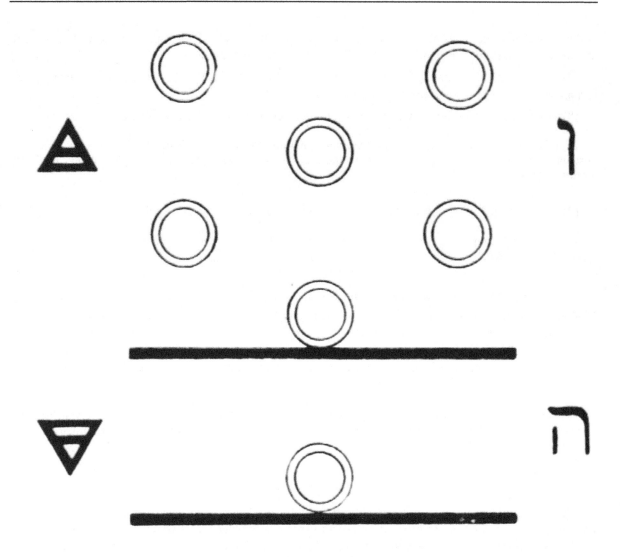

Plate 4: The Four Planes of the Tree of Life

Plate 4: The Three Pillars of the Tree of Life The active mood of the Divine Light enters the right-hand pillar through 'Hokmah, and the passive mood enters through Binah, the union of these two lights creating the central pillar, the Word or Logos. The formulation of this Word, by balancing the moods of Light, constitutes the Great Magical Work of the Qabalah.

To the student of the occult it will be apparent that these two trees closely resemble the letter Shin, also the caduceus of Hermes with its central rod and its two entwined serpents, and also the Ida, Pingala, and central Shushumna of Hindu Yoga. The whole scheme is symbolized in the Temple of Solomon, the temple itself being the central pillar, whilst its two pylons, Yakhin and Boaz, the white and the black, the right and the left, represent the Tree of the Knowledge of Good and Evil - the eternal complementary forces in life without which nothing can be. This symbolism is an excessively ancient one thus, in the Norse Mythology we find the mystic tree Yggdrasil, the roots of which are in the material world and the branches of which reach up to Asgard, the happy dwelling of the gods. Again, amongst the Akkadians, Chaldeans, and Babylonians we find the World Tree, or Tree of Life, which "stood mid-way between the Deep and Zikum" - the primordial heaven above. In Hindu mythology there is also a World Tree - the Lingam-and in Buddhist the Bodhi Tree, or Tree of Wisdom under which Buddha sat in meditation. Finally, that masterpiece of Gothic architecture the cathedral probably finds its origin in the tree-trunks and overhanging branches of the forest glade.

The Four Worlds

Thus far the Sephirotic Scheme may be considered as simple, but in its extended form it grows complex; for not only is the Tree of Life divided into three planes which become four in Malkuth, but it is projected from the Godhead through four worlds each containing a Tree of ten Sephiroth, and each Sephirah containing within itself ten of these intelligences, each of which is threefold in nature for as it is written: "Just as the Ancient is represented by the number three, so are all the other lights of a threefold nature." [21] In all there are, therefore, 400 Sephiroth in the world scheme, and as 400 is the numerical value of u, *Tau*,Th, the last letter of the Hebrew alphabet, 400 completes the cycle of the creative Voice or Logos.

As the threefold order is intellectually important, so is the fourfold order physically important, the two multiplied together making 12 and representing the Zodiac (see Plate V on page 34), the twelve months of the Year, etc., and consequently the entire creative cycle symbolized by two interlaced six-pointed stars or Seals of Solomon; the one being the Great Work below and the other the Great Work above.

There are four Manifestations - the No-Thing, the Intellectual World, the Sensuous World, and the Physical World; also the four elements Air, Fire, Water, and Earth, the four Living Beasts of the Chariot Throne, and the four letters in the name of Tetragrammaton. In the *Zohar* we read:

The firmament is imprinted, at the four corners of a square, with four figures, of a lion, an eagle, an ox, and a man; and the face of a man is traced in all of them, so that the face of Lion is of Man, the face of Eagle is of Man, and the face of Ox is of Man, all being comprehended in him. [22]

Hence the four great Qabalistic Worlds together form a unit, a single Great Man, the Macrocosm or Adam Illaah, the Archetypal Man - the Form of the Universe through which is manifested the Divine Essence of the Ain Soph. Their names are:

(I) Atziluth or the Atziluthic World, the Archetypal World or World of Emanations - the ten Sephiroth of which represent the operative qualities of the Divine Will. This world is also called the Great Seal, for it stamps out in its own form the three inferior worlds. It is the abode of Adam Qadmon.

(2) Briah or the Briatic World, the World of Creation - the ten Sephiroth of which represent the abode of pure spirits; consequently it contains no matter. It is the dwelling of the Angel Metatron and constitutes the World of Angels or Spirits. As Adam Qadmon is the form of the Ain Soph, Metatron is his garment and under his command come the myriads of the angelic hosts of the next world.

Plate 5: The Zodiacal

(3)   Yetzirah or the Yetziratic World, the World of Formation - the ten Sephiroth of which represent the Angels or Intelligences of the stars and planets. The *Zohar* says:

For the Servants [Sephiroth] that serve the Holy, Blessed be He! It made the Throne [the Briatic World], and four supports [Pillar of Mildness] and six steps [Pillars of Mercy and Justice] to the Throne, together ten. The whole is like a cup of blessing. (See Diagram 2.)

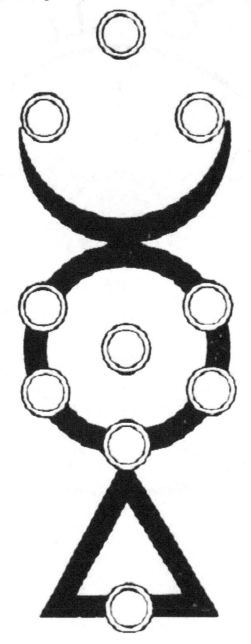

Diagram 2: The Qabalistic Chalice

That which is in the ten words, like the Thorah which is given in ten words; and as the universe, which is the Maaseh Beraishith, which has been created by ten sayings. The Holy, Blessed be He! affixed to the Throne legions to serve it [the Ten Angelic Hosts of this World]. . . . And for the service of these, the Holy, Blessed be He! made Sammael and his legions, who are as it were the clouds to be used to come down upon the earth. And they are the horses: and above the cloud is the Merkabah, the Chariot Throne, therefore it is said *[Isaiah* xix, I]: "Behold YHVH rideth upon a swift cloud and shall come into Mitsraim [Egypt]." And so the Holy, Blessed be He! rules Mitsraim. [23]

This world is seemingly the abode of Tetragrammaton.

(4) Assiah or the Assiatic World, the World of Action, also called the World of Qliphoth, that is the World of Shells or Demons. In its ten Sephiroth lives the actual material substance of the universe. It is the abode of Sammael, the Prince of Darkness.

It is subject to change, birth, death, corruption and re-birth, yet not anything in it is considered as ever totally annihilated or destroyed in essence or atom. It is the abode of the Evil Spirit and his demonical forces. [24]

Such are the four worlds. In the simple Sephirotic Scheme the first is referred to Kether, 'Hokmah, and Binah; the second to 'Hesed, Pahad, and Tiphereth; the third to Netzah, Hod, and Yesod; and the fourth to affixed to the Throne legions to serve it [the Ten Angelic Hosts of this World]. . . And for the service of these, the Holy, Blessed be He! made Sammael and his legions, who are as it were the clouds to be used to come down upon the earth. And they are the horses: and above the cloud is the Merkabah, the Chariot Throne, therefore it is said *[Isaiah xix,* i]: "Behold YHVH rideth upon a swift cloud and shall come into Mitsraim [Egypt]." And so the Holy, Blessed be He! rules Mitsraim. [25] This world is seemingly the abode of Tetragrammaton.

Such are the four worlds. In the simple Sephirotic Scheme the first is referred to Kether, 'Hokmah, and Binah; the second to 'Hesed, Pahad, and Tiphereth; the third to Netzah, Hod, and Yesod; and the fourth to Malkuth. Also, in *Genesis* i, "Let there be Light" refers to the Atziluthic World; "Elohim saw the light, that it was good" refers to the Briatic World; "Elohim divided the light from the darkness" refers to the Yetziratic World; and "Elohim called the light Day, and the darkness he called Night" refers to the Assiatic World. Thus the whole process of creation is the evolution of Light: from an absolute quality to a tangible quality; from what is incomprehensible to what is comprehensible; from what is from God and beyond man to what is of God and within man; for all and everything is Light in varying forms of density or purity. From Light we come and unto Light we go; the great Qabalistic secret being the transmutation of Darkness, light in its material form into illuminism, that is Light in its spiritual form. Such is the Grand Telesma of the World.

CHAPTER III

THE PROBLEM OF GOOD AND EVIL

Good and Evil.

THUS far we have dealt with the theory of the Qabalah in its exoteric, philosophical, and cosmological forms: now we shall enter more and more deeply into its esoteric spirit. We shall meet with many contradictions, for the Qabalah is full of gropings in opposite directions; yet in the end, for the greater part, they cancel each other out, leaving to the searcher after truth a clear illuminating picture.

We start with the archetypal, the world as an idea, a thought, a mathematical conception such as space, which contains all things. To this idea we add a creative impulse, and the world is endowed with a will to unfold itself and we enter the sphere of time, of thought in extension. From this unfolding emerges form - geometricity, or a multiplication of spaces, shadows of things to be. So far there is no materiality; only mathematics, numbers, and letters; symbols, of shapes which are still dreaming. Lastly, in these forms movement is born and they become what we call substantial; then only do we enter the physical world of action - of materialized thought.

Movement presupposes a working outwards from a centre, or a working inwards from a circumference, a breathing in and out. In both there is a starting-point and a beyond the starting-point: a duality which presupposes a choice between at least two directions, the value of each differing according to the circumstances which surround each at any given time. Consequently in the intellectual sphere there must always be a right and a wrong path of action; in the moral sphere a good and a bad path; and in the physical sphere one which gains or loses, assists or resists.

These three series of opposite but, in reality, complementary principles have ever since the beginnings of human thought perplexed the mind of man, and none more so than the second, which has revolved round the problem of good and evil. Deeply and searchingly has the Qabalist meditated upon this problem, until Wisdom revealed to him that the World of Action is fashioned of two distinct yet inseparable elements: the positive life-giving principle which reveals itself as energy, and the negative death-giving principle which reveals itself as inertia. To him the first is spiritual and the second material. The one he symbolizes by the hosts of angels and the other by the evil spirits of the Qliphoth. Isaac Myer explains this very clearly when he writes:

The Qabbalah does not recognize in the Good and Evil, two independent, automatic, opposing powers, but both are, according to it, under the power of the Supreme Absolute Deity. It asserts that the Evil springs out of the Good, and only originated from a diversion of the latter. Evil exists, for God's own wise purpose, by the sufferance of the Absolute One, who gives us the blighting cold, frost, and night, and also the beneficent and blessed daylight, warmth, and sunshine. Man therefore partakes of two regions, that of the external, visible, matter world, that of Evil and Darkness, and that of the internal spiritual higher world, that of Goodness and Light.

The German Philosopher Hegel holds that a thing can only *exist* through its opposite, *that the thing and its opposite must arise together, and that eternally, as the complements of a unity;* white is not without black, nor black without white, good is not without, nor *is* evil without good. This is the doctrine of the Siphrah D'Tzinoothah and the Sepher Ye'tzeer-ah. At the very beginning of the life germ, dissolution and death oppose its vitality and endeavour to destroy it, and the whole existence of man in this world is a continual struggle to preserve his vitality. Isaiah says, in his magnificent language: "I am YHVH, and there is none else, there is not any Elohim besides Me. I girded thee, though thou hast not known Me; that they may know from the rising of the sun, and from the west, that there is none beside Me. I am YHVH, and there is none else. I from light create darkness; I make safety and I create misfortune; I YHVH do all these things." [1]

Isaiah's words are pure Qabalah; for instance in the *Zohar* we read: "Observe", he said, "that the Holy One, blessed be He, made a Right and a Left for the ruling of the world. The one is called 'good', and the other 'evil', and He made man to be a combination of the two." [2]

And again:

When the Holy One, blessed be He, created the world, He created it by means of the letters of the Torah, all the letters of the Alphabet having presented themselves before Him until finally the letter Beth was chosen for the starting point. . . . But when it came to the turn of the Teth and the Resh to present themselves together, the Teth refused to take its place; so God chid it, saying: "0 Teth, Teth, why, having come up, art thou loth to take thy place?" It replied: "Seeing that Thou hast placed me at the head of *tob* (good), how can I associate with the Resh, the initial of ra' (evil)?" God thereupon said to it: "Go to thy place, as thou hast need of the Resh. For man, whom I am about to create, will be composed of you both, but thou wilt be on his right whilst the other will be on his left." [3]

In the *Book of Genesis* this duality in man is hidden in the words "Let us make man in our image", that is in light; "after our likeness" (simulacrum or shadow), that is in darkness, which is the garment of light.

The purpose of evil is to stimulate goodness.

.....The Holy One inflicts suffering on the righteous in this world in order that they may merit the world to come. But he who is weak of soul and strong of body is hated of God. It is because God has no pleasure in him that He inflicts no pain upon him in this world, but permits his life to flow smoothly along with ease and comfort, in that for any virtuous act he may perform he receives his reward in this world, so that no portion should be left him in the next world.[4]

Again:

All the acts of the Almighty are in accordance with justice, and His purpose is to purify that soul from the scum that adheres to it in this world, so as to bring it into the world to come. [5]

Here, mildly though it may be, we are introduced to the pernicious doctrine of Manichaeism, which is still further accentuated in the following quotation:

Every man has a foretaste of death during the night, because the holy soul then leaves him, and the unclean spirit rests on the body and makes it unclean. When, however, the soul returns to the body, the pollution disappears, save from the man's hands, which retain it and thus remain unclean. Hence a man should not pass his hands over his eyes before washing them [the open eye symbolizes Kether]. When he has washed them, however, he becomes sanctified and is called holy. For this sanctification two vessels are required, one held above and the other placed beneath, so that he may be sanctified by the water poured on his hands from the vessel above. The lower vessel, then, is the vessel of uncleanness . . . [whilst the upper vessel is a medium of sanctification] [6]

Between these opposites of good and evil is placed the free will of man, which establishes harmony between them and by which man exercises the divine power of judgment. Man is, therefore, a living representative of the Tree of Life, or conversely the Tree of Life is a pictorial representation of man. To the Tree of Life each Sephirah is both good and evil: good in its relation to the Sephirah immediately above it, and evil in its relation to the Sephirah immediately below it. In the *Sepher Yetzirah* we read

The ineffable Sephiroth . . . they are . . . the infinity of the Beginning and the infinity of the End, the infinity of the Good and the infinity of the Evil. [7]

And again:

Twenty-two basal letters; they are placed together in a ring, as a wall with two hundred and thirty-one gates. The ring may be put in rotation forwards or backwards and its token is this: Nothing excels gno = ONG (= pleasure) in good, and nothing excels ogn = NGO (= plague) in evil. [8]

In man good and evil represent the pillars of Mercy and Severity (or Justice), whilst free will represents the central pillar of Mildness.

This mystery of good, will, and evil is the foundation of the symbolical Temple of Solomon. Myer writes:

The widow's son, Hiram Abiff of Tyre, cast for the Qabalistic Temple of King Solomon two high pillars or pylons of bronze; their capitals were pomegranates and lily work. The lily, most likely the lotus, an emblem of life, white or male, on the right side, the pomegranate, the emblem of fecundity and plasticity, red or female, on the left side. The first was called Yakheen, the latter Boaz. These columns represented, Understanding, Binah, h, and Wisdom, 'Hokhmah, v, and between them was the Temple of Kether, y, the Father. Here we see symbols of the Former, the Harmony, and the to be Formed. All energy must have resistance, all light must have darkness, all projecture or emanation, a hollow or excavation to receive efflux. Affirmation supposes a negation; if the first androgene had not been separated into male and female, the result would have been entire sterility, as was the result as to the Seven Kings of Edom described in Genesis and the Qabbalah; and the Balance not existing, the forms did not and could not exist, and the emanation of the existences could not proceed and be manifest. [9]

Sympathy and antipathy governed by harmony is the secret not only of the spiritual but of the moral and physical worlds. The letters ∞*od, Heh,* and *Vau* are their symbols, and together they form YHV (Gnostic lAO), the ineffable name. This symbolism is universal because it is universally true. In the Zodiac, Scorpio, male, and Virgo, female, are united by Libra, the balance. The three divine essentials are Necessity and Liberty linked together by Harmony. Truth cannot exist without doubt, hope without fear, life without death; and so we find that, whatever the attempted explanation is, good and evil are necessary one to the other just as are the centripetal and centrifugal forces of the heavenly bodies. Everywhere are they to be found except in the Absolute, where all comes to rest in NoThingness.

In this duality of good and evil the danger is that the uninitiated see two separate unities: they see good as God and evil as Satan. Consequently they love the one and hate the other, and so establish a disunity within and among themselves. This is the foundation of Manichaeism. They cannot see, as the Mishna says, that "God has placed in all things one to oppose the other" and that "good purifies evil and evil purifies good" [10]. This is the essential ignorance which Separates Christianity from Judaism; for to the Christians salvation consists in the conquest of evil - that is, in its separation from the good.

The Evolution of Satan.

The personification of evil in the form of Satan as the God of Evil is the heresy which separates Christianity from Judaism; consequently, in order to understand what this heresy entails, it is of vital importance to enquire into the nature of the Hebrew Sammael, the genius of the Yetziratic World, the world of Angels, that is of Intelligences. This task is a highly complex one, for it is wrapped up in the principle of necessity, because outside the No-Thing, Deity is not a free agent.

As we have seen in the last chapter, Adam Qadmon - that is Deity in the form of the Archetypal Man, the Great Seal, and consequently the Great Mystery - by a process of inversion, that is of fall or reflection, be-comes Metatron in the Briatic World; and then Metatron by a similar process becomes Sammael in the Yetziratic World. In this world Sammael's clouds of angels are the horses of Tetragrammaton which bring YHVH into Egypt, that is into the Assiatic World, for Egypt typifies darkness. His Chariot is the Merkabah (Throne of Magic); Tetragrammaton is the Charioteer; and as his two horses (two categories of Angels) typify good and evil, (the white and the black or the white and the red) Tetragrammaton himself represents the fall of Yetziratic Harmony. In fact, the symbolism here describes the descent of the Tree of Life into Assiah, where it is reversed and changed from Harmony into Discord - that is into Activity.

Why should this descent take place? The answer is "of necessity". Tetragrammaton must descend, because only by descending can he complete the cycle of emanations and so ultimately (through a reversed process of emanation) reinstate the No-Thingness of the Ayin. As we have shown, the first fall is from the Ain Soph to Adam Qadmon, the second from Adam Qadmon to Metatron, the third from Metatron to Sammael, and the fourth from the angelic Sammael to his demoniacal counterpart; for we are told that "Life in the present dispensation is cut short through the influence of the evil serpent, whose dominion is symbolized by the darkened moon". [11] The mention of the "Evil Serpent" presupposes the existence of a "Good Serpent" - the Serpent of Yetzirah.

To simplify this problem it is necessary to enter more deeply into the idea of the Fall. Sammael of necessity revolts against Deity, as symbolized by Metatron, and of necessity he is cast out of heaven - that is out of the Yetziratic World. In the Assiatic World, the World of Matter, in order to redeem himself, of necessity he has to tempt the earthly Adam. His task there is to cause death, that is to reverse the life process; as the *Zohar* says, "the end of all flesh has come before Me [Sammael]"; for he, as the Evil Serpent, "takes away the souls of all flesh", [12] that is he liberates them from matter. He is called the Angel of Venom, of Poison, of Death; for *Sam* means "poison" and *El* means "angel". His number is 131, that is trinity set between two unities, the whole adding up to 5 - the Microcosm.

His world is now the Yetziratic World reversed; that is to say Assiah is the simulacrum, shadow, or image, of Yetzirah. Its three supernal Sephiroth are Tohu, the Formless, Bohu, the Void, and ChShK - Darkness. Its seven lower Sephiroth are seven hells. Each of these ten Infernal Sephiroth is inhabited by a host of demons, of which the first two orders are without form, the third is of darkness, and the remaining seven represent all human vices (activities).

These seven infernal halls [or hells] are sub-divided into endless compartments, so as to afford a separate chamber of torture for every species of sin. The prince of this region of darkness is called Satan in the Bible. . . He is the same evil spirit, Satan, the Serpent, who seduced Eve. [13]

We are also told that:

The Ten Sephiroth of Atziluth have scintillated and brought forth the Ten Sephiroth of Briah, and from the energy of these Ten of Briah sparkled forth the scintillations of the World Yetzirah, and through these the Ten Sephiroth of the World Assiah were sealed. [14]

These are the Seals of St. John's *Apocalypse.*

Thus it is disclosed to us that the God of Assiah is the reversed Sammael of Yetzirah, who is the reversed Metatron of Briah, who is the reversed Adam Qadmon of Atziluth. In brief, Sammael in Assiah is the reversed Adam Qadmon three times removed; he is the "dark shadow of the manifestation of the Great Androgene of Good". [15] He is Metatron in an active form, just as when in Yetzirah he is Metatron in a passive form - the Serpent Above and the Serpent Below. He is Tetragrammaton reversed; and this was grasped by Picus de Mirandula when he wrote in his *Kabbalistic Conclusions.*

The letters of the name of the evil demon who is the prince of this world are the same as those of the name of God – Tetragrammaton - and he who knows how to effect their transposition can extract one from the other. [16]

In brief, as the sorcerers were wont to proclaim:

Daemon est Deus inversus.

Like Adam Qadmon, the evil Sammael is androgenous, for his female companion, or counterpart, is Esheth Zenunim (AShTh[17] ZNVNIM) the Harlot, or Woman of Whoredom, also called Lilith, which name signifies "night". Sammael is the active principle, Lilith the passive; in union they formulate the Antichrist, Anti-Logos, or Anti-Word, known under the name of 'Hay-yah [18] the Beast, [19] the numerical value of which is 25, that is one unit less than the numerical value of Tetragrammaton, which is 26. One is the numerical value of *Aleph*, a , hence in Omar Khayyám we read:

A Hair perhaps divides the False and True;
Yes; and a single Alif were the clue- Could
you but find it-to the Treasure-house, And
peradventure to The Master too.

This mystery is solved as follows: Aleph is composed of two ∞odin and a cross-bar which is a Vau. It represents the World Above separated from the World Below by the Vital Force; its value is consequently $10 + 6 + 10 = 26$, and 26 is the numerical value of Tetragrammaton. Its symbols are also the Swastika, Fylfot, or Gammadion. (See Plate VI on page 42.)

The redemption from Satanic rule can only be attained by seeing God as He really is and not as He is in his reflection; for as Éliphas Lévi writes:

According to the Kabalists, the true name of Satan is that of Jehovah reversed, for Satan is not a black god but the negation of the Deity. He is the personification of atheism and idolatry. The Devil is not a personality for initiates, but a force created with a good object, though it can be applied to evil: it is really the instrument of liberty. [20]

To God the reflection of Himself is evil, but to man this reflection is good, so long as he does not attempt to emulate God by reflecting his own personal Shekinah *(Shin,* w), or soul, on the chaos of human ignorance, that is on the unbalanced minds of those who surround him. In order to do so righteously, this chaos must first be stilled so that it may become a luminous mirror capable of reflecting the glory of the Shekinah in all its perfection. In the past, the diabolical error made even by some of the greatest masters and the most illumined adepts was that, when once they had reduced their consciousness to zero, and on the mirror thus created had received the reflection of the Shekinah, they attempted to reflect this reflection on the unpurified minds of their followers. The result was not illuminism but madness, not for them only, but for those intoxicated by them.

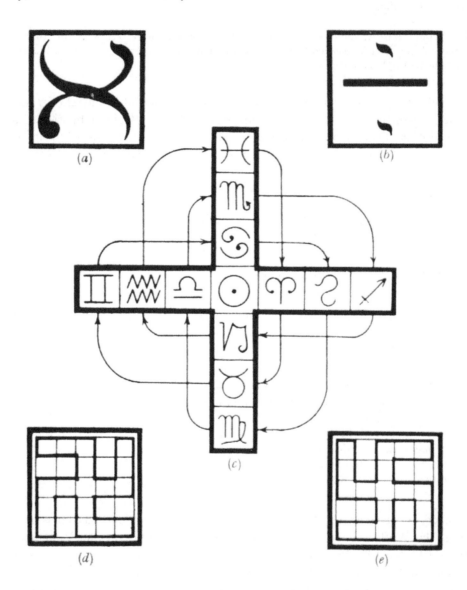

(a) Aleph; (b) the beginning of motion through opposition; *(c)* the whirling forces of the Zodiac; *(d)* the female Swastika; *(e)* the male Swastika. The 17 squares of the Swastika refer to IAO, whose numerical value is 17.

Plate 6: The Mystery of Aleph

In the first chapter of *Genesis* is depicted the fall of the Yetziratic Deity through inversion due to reflection; the glory of this Deity, that is the Shekinah within it, being the agent which renders the formation of a simulacrum possible. According to the Zohar, Metatron "sets all his legions in motion by the power of a single letter [Shin]".[21] This was the spoken word Tetragrammaton, which created Light, when the Yetziratic emanation moved upon the face of the waters (the luminous mirror) and proclaimed "Yehe Aur" (value 222), "Let there be Light" (Illumination). In proclaiming it, the Shekinah, Astral Light, Ether, or by whatever name the reader chooses to call it, emerged from out of the Yetziratic Deity, leaving the four Tetragrammatic letters of his name reflected upon the deep. These four letters represent what may be called the materiality of this Deity, the elements of air, fire, water, and earth. In themselves they are not spiritual but are reflected upon spirit, the *Shin* by going forth from the Yetziratic Deity rendering them visible.

This transmutation of Tetragrammaton - or the despiritualized good Sammael - into matter is one of the profoundest mysteries of the Qabalah, a mystery so secret that it is nowhere clearly explained. We are told that the name of Tetragrammaton is unpronounceable, and this in fact is so, for though YHVH can be pronounced as Yahweh, or Jehovah, this is not the true name of Tetragrammaton, for his name must contain the Shekinah as symbolized by the letter *Shin*. If this letter is placed in the centre of the four letters of Tetragrammaton, we obtain YHShVH; that is Ishvah, Yeheshua, Jehoshuar, Joshua, and Jesus, any one of which may be taken as the veritable name of the Yetziratic Deity, the God or Genius of the World of Formation. The Chief of the Angelic Hosts is YHwVH (=326 = 11 = 5 + 6 = the Microcosm and the Macrocosm), and only when the Shekinah (w) flames forth does Tetragrammaton descend in the Merkabah, the Chariot of Magic, and become the Great Magician of the earthly world.

To translate this involved symbolism in a simple way: GOD becomes manifest to our consciousness through the vibrations of light, life, love, etc. - His Spirit. This manifestation is nevertheless not God but the reflection of God on these vibrations; consequently, of necessity, it must be reversed and becomes DOG. [22]

The Problem of Free Will.

It is apparent that the centre of this problem is the letter Shin, the most mysterious in the Hebrew alphabet. Its sound is like the hiss of a Serpent, its appearance that of the open mouth of a snake (jaws and tongue), and its numerical value clearly shows its triadic nature; further still, 300, its value, esoterically symbolizes the 300 Sephiroth of the three Worlds which preceded the creation of the World of Matter.

Though as Spiritual fire, or glory, it is the symbol of the Shekinah, the *Sepher Yetzirah* hints that it also represents transmutation and the Devil.[23] Usually the thirty-first path of the Tree of Life is referred to it, and according to *The 32 Paths of Wisdom,* this path "is called the Perpetual Intelligence. . . . Because it rules the movement of the sun and the moon according to their constitution, and causes each to gravitate in its respective orb". [24] In other words, it is the equilibrating force in the World of Action, Kether, 'Hokmah, and Binah, Christ and the two thieves on their crosses, the caduceus of Hermes, the solar disc and dual serpents of Egypt, and, according to Éliphas Lévi, the Astral Light between the horns of the Baphomet of Mendes - the Panlike Satan of the Templars. When erect it is the rod of Aaron and the Brazen Serpent of Moses. (See Plate VII on page 44.) Its three teeth, or tongues, represent three *Vaudin* and consequently may be translated into the number 666, the solar number and the number of the Beast in the *Apocalypse*. According to the *Siphrah D'Tzniuthah*, it is The Serpent which runs with 370 leaps. [25] It "leaps over mountains and hastily runs up over hills". . . . . . . The Serpent holds its tail in its mouth with its teeth. It is perforated on both sides. When the Perfect One [or the Archangel Metatron?] is raised up, the Serpent is changed into three spirits. [26]

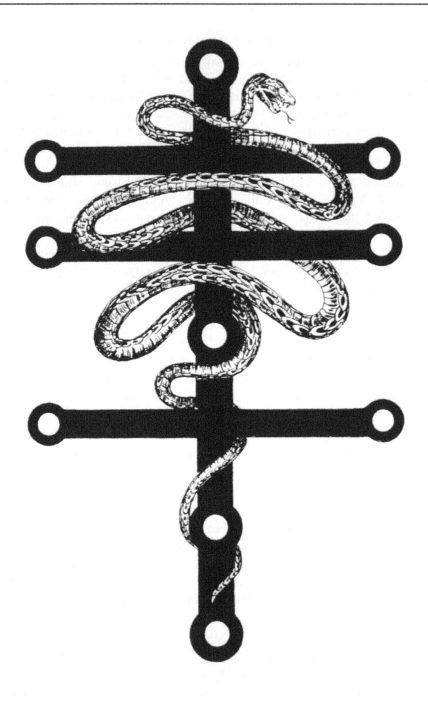

Plate 7: The Brazen Serpent It is energy and the order within energy - the Balance of the Forces. Isaac Myer writes

The harmony is represented by the circle, by the serpent, an emblem of both Satan and Wisdom, with its tail in its mouth. In the physical universe it is the luminiferous aether, the vital caloric, the electro-magnetic azoth. It is the ambient fluid which penetrates, permeates, vitalizes all Things, the ray detached from the glory of the sun, fixed by the weight of the atmosphere, and crystallized by the central attraction, to our earth. In the words of the erudite Yehudah ha-Levi (A.D. 1140): "There is not any life without motion, nor motion without inspiration, no inspiration without struggle, no struggle without opposition; oppositions are everywhere essential, but the Divine power conciliates every opposition." *(Sepher Khozari,* Part IV, para. 25.) [27]

Satan, as we call this power, is in fact the Tree of Life of our world, that free will which for its very existence depends on the clash of the positive and negative forces which in the moral sphere we call good and evil. Satan is therefore the Shekinah of Assiah, the World of Action, the perpetual activity of the Divine Essence, the Light which was created on the first day and which in the form of consciousness and intelligence can produce an overpowering brilliance equal to the intensest darkness. Satan is also the Flaming Sword which brought light from heaven. (See Diagram 3.)

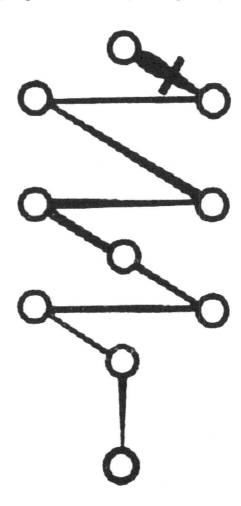

Diagram 3: The Flaming Sword

The understanding of this power, whether in the physical, moral, or intellectual planes, is called science, and the misunderstanding of it is frequently called magic. As magician, Sammael is preeminently the Poison-God. "There is more than one Sammael," says the *Zohar,* "and they are not all equal, but this side of the serpent is accursed above all of them." [28]

In man the will is the magician; when it tends towards evil it is called black, when towards good it is called white; but when it tends towards neither and in place harmonizes both, then it manifests not as the magician but as the Shekinah, the Vital Force as Harmonizing Agent, Hermes the messenger of God.

The Mystery of Sex.

The problem of sex, being a problem of duality, is closely connected in the Qabalah with that of good and evil. It is looked upon as the great cosmological mystery, for marriage is the symbol of perfect harmony. As the Zohar says:

The words "male and female he created them" make known the high dignity of man, the mystic doctrine of his creation. . . . From this we learn that every figure which does not comprise male and female elements is not a true and proper figure. [29]

And again:

He who dies without leaving children will not enter within the curtain of heaven and will have no share in the other world, and his soul will not be admitted to the place where all souls are gathered, and his image will be cut off from there.

Why? Because "he has not succeeded in radiating light in this world by the means of the body". [30]

The creation of life is man's divine prerogative; consequently the sex act is of all acts the holiest. According to the *Nobeleth 'Hokhmah*:

The Qabbalists say that the entering into existence of the worlds happened through delight, in that Ain Soph rejoiced in Itself and flashed and beamed from Itself to Itself; and from these intelligent movements and spiritual and divine scintillations, from the parts of Its being to Its being, which are called delight, Its sources have spread themselves towards the outside, as seeds for the world. [31]

Here is described to us the sublime orgasm of the Ain Soph, the creation through Bliss. So also it is with man and woman:

"0 that his left hand were under my head, and his right hand should embrace me" (S.S. ii, 6). Then male and female are united, and there is mutual desire and worlds are blessed and upper and lower rejoice. [32]

Then we are told that "The most perfect form of praising God is to unify the Holy Name in the fitting manner". [33] What is this? It is in such a manner that the complementary forces symbolized in it may manifest their creative powers. Thus in the name of YHVH we find two dualities, one between the ∞od and the *Heh* (Father and Mother) and the other between the *Vau* and the *Heh* (Son and Daughter). Without the *Heh* the Father is inconceivable and without the ∞od the Mother is inconceivable. What is conceivable is always a relationship; not ∞od in itself nor *Heh* in itself, but

∞od *Heh* in conjunction. ∞od, be it remembered, has the numerical value of 10 and thus holds within itself the seed of the Tree of Life. The value of *Heh* being 5, this letter represents the Microcosmic power which can bring the Sephirotic Scheme into consciousness. Again, in order to realize the perfection of the unity of ∞od *Heh* it is necessary to establish a unity between *Vau* and *Heh*. Here the *Vau,* which is of the value 6, represents the consciousness of the Macrocosm and *Heh* the Microcosmic power, not in God but in man.

In the *Zohar* we find a complex account of these permutations, which is worth quoting. It reads as follows:

Before Israel went into captivity, and while the Shekinah was still with them, God commanded Israel: "thou shalt not uncover thy mother's nakedness" (Lev. xviii, 7), and this captivity is the uncovering of the nakedness of the Shekinah, as it is written, "On account of your sins your mother has been put away" (Is. 1, i), i.e. for the sin of unchastity Israel has been sent into captivity and the Shekinah also, and this is the uncovering of the Shekinah. This unchastity is Lilith, the mother of the "mixed multitude". It Is they who separate the two He's of the sacred name, and prevent the Vau from entering between them; so it is written "the nakedness of a woman and her daughter thou shalt not uncover", referring to the upper and lower Shekinah. When the "mixed multitude" are between the one Hé and the other, the Holy One, blessed be He, cannot link them together, and consequently "the river becomes dry and parched" - dry in the upper Hé and parched in the lower Hé, in order that the "mixed multitude" may not be nourished by the Vau, which is the Tree of Life [the ∞od extended]. Therefore the Vau does not link together the two Hé's when the mixed multitude is between them, and the letter ∞od is not able to draw near to the second Hé; thus the precept "thou shalt not uncover the nakedness of thy daughter-in-law" is transgressed. Further, they separate the ∞od from the upper Hé, and so break the command "thou shalt not uncover the nakedness of thy father's wife", the ∞od being the father, the first Hé the mother, Vau the son and the second Hé the daughter. Therefore it is ordained with regard to the upper Hé, "thou shalt not uncover the nakedness of thy father's wife"; "the nakedness of thy sister the daughter of thy father" refers to the lower Hé; "her son's daughter to her daughter's daughter" refers to the Hé and Hé which are the children of

Hé; "the nakedness of the father's brother" refers to the ∞od, which is the product of the letter ∞od, a brother to Vau. In a word, when the "mixed multitude" are mingled with Israel, the letters of the name YHVH cannot be joined and linked together; but as soon as they are removed from the world, then it is said of the letters of God's name that "On that day the Lord shall be one and his name one" (Zech. xiv, 9). 34

As in God above all things become a perfect unity, that is a perfect balance, so also in man below must a perfect unity be established, for all things are also to be found in man. To the Qabalist the mystery of faith consists "in the union of God with the female whom He fructifies, after the manner of the union of male and female". To the Christian this may seem a blasphemy, but remembering that in the Qabalah the union of the sexes is looked upon as the sublimest act in life, to the Jews it is the reverse. "Benediction does not abide save when male and female are together" ; [35] and even Moses the Law-giver of Israel was not considered perfect because he was separated from his wife. [36] God being a unity in the spiritual world, this oneness is manifested in the material world when the male is united to the female "in a righteous purpose" [37]; for it is through the union of bodies and souls that perfect unity is attained.

So long as Jacob was unmarried, God did not manifest to him clearly. . . . After marriage he arrived at the perfection which is above as distinguished from the perfection which is below, and God manifested to him clearly. [38]

We thus see that the mystery of sex is but the mystery of good and evil looked at from another angle. And as in the first problem the separation of evil from good is the main cause of differentiation between Christian and Hebrew ethics, so is the looking upon the sex act as sinful in place of righteous the main cause of differentiation between Christian and Hebrew morality. As Christian Ginsburg writes:

Love and fear are designed to aid the soul in achieving her high destiny, when she shall no more look through the dark glass, but see face to face in the presence of the Luminous Mirror, by permeating all acts of obedience and divine worship. [39]

CHAPTER IV

THE FALL OF TETRAGRMMMATON

The Principles of Creation.

When discussing the philosophy of the Qabalah, we touched upon the principles of creation; here we will return to this subject, for they constitute the foundations of mystic knowledge towards which, as we shall show later on, scientific thought is tending.

First it must be realized that though, in the ordinary use of words, creation conveys to us an idea of "springing up", that is of newness and novelty, to the Qabalist it conveys the opposite idea, namely, that of descending, obscuring, and grossifying. For instance, no rational being would assert that a work of art was greater than the artist who created it. A statue is an artistic idea materialized. It is of stone, clay, or metal - pure matter - to which has been added an ideal form which emanated from the thoughts of a human being also fashioned of matter, that is of flesh, blood, and bone. It was not thought which created the material of the statue, for this existed before the thought arose in the head of the artist; yet thought did give to the statue its form, and this crystallized thought may live on long after the flesh, blood, and bone of the artist have fallen to dust. Will the artist, then, have perished? No, not altogether, for he will in part live on in the form of the statue which perhaps for thousands of years will proclaim his genius to those who look upon it.

With the entire world, the entire universe, it is the same, but with this difference: it expresses the totality of the thoughts of the Divine Thinker. Thought, we have seen, gave it form; therefore the universe is God in form and in activity. "All that has been created," says the *Zohar*, "from the Holy Beasts [the Kerubim] in the highest firmament, down to the tiniest worm that crawls upon the earth, lives in Elohim and through Elohim." [1] That is to say, everything which is, has been, or will be is formed by the Divine Thought; therefore the universe is the symbol of the Divine Thinker.

What is it formed of? What is the material? The void and the formless, the negative and the positive of vhb, Bohu (BHV), and vhu, Tohu (ThHV), which find their Harmony in the Darkness. And be it noted that *Beth*, the first letter of BHV, is the letter of creation, the first letter of *Genesis*, and that it represents the open mouth, or parted lips, which utter the Logoic Word. Also that as *Tau*, the first letter of ThHV, is the final letter of the Hebrew alphabet, it completes the utterance, and as its numerical value is 400 it represents the 400 Sephiroth of the four worlds. Finally, that each word includes a *Heh* and a *Vau*, a feminine and a masculine quantity, and that the numerical values of these four letters is 22 - the number of letters in the Hebrew alphabet; consequently, potentially, the names of all things (forms) are included in them.

These two find their equilibrium in Darkness or the black fire.

Tohu [we are told] is under the aegis of *Shaddai*; *Bohu*, under that of *Zebaoth*; Darkness, under that of *Elohim*; Spirit, under that of YHVH. . . . "There was a strong wind breaking the mountains, but the Lord was not in the wind", because this name was not in it, since *Shaddai* presides over it through the mystic nature of *Tohu*. "After the wind there was a quaking, but the Lord was not in the quaking", since over it presides the name of Zebaoth, through the mystic nature of *Bohu* (which is called quaking [ra'ash], because it quakes continually). "After the quaking there was a fire, but the Lord was not in the fire", because over it presides the name *Elohim* from the side of darkness. "And after the fire there was a small still voice"; and here at last was found the name YHVH. [2]

This small still voice represents the *Shin* emerging from YHShVH, which by turning the darkness into a luminous mirror enabled YHVH to be reflected upon it. Then only was the Balance between the Former and the Formless established. As the divine spark scintillated forth, "He caused a wind to blow from above against a wind that blew from below. From the shock of the meeting of these two winds, a *Drop* emerged and rose from the depths of the abyss. This Drop united the winds and from the union of these winds the world was born", [3] a simulacrum of Elohim - Who? . . . These ! - in which the form of every atom represents a divine idea.

Or we may try to understand it in another way: The Indivisible Point or *Supreme Point* sends forth a light of such transparency, limpidity and subtlety that it penetrates everywhere. Around the Point, the penetration of its own light forms a ring or a Palace. The light of the *Supreme Point* being of an inconceivable brilliance, the light of the Palace which is inferior to it looks like a dark circle round it. But the light of the First Palace, though it may seem dark by comparison with the Point itself, is yet of an immense splendour which gives off another ring or palace forming a sort of envelope around the first one. So that, emanating from the *Supreme Point*, all the degrees of creation are but envelopes, the one for the other. The envelope of the superior degree forms the *brain* of the degree next to it. [4]

Here is presented to us a system of worlds within worlds. First there is the world, or expanse, of No-Thingness; then the Awir, or ether; next the Aur, or light; then ten Sephirotic rings of light, one grosser than the other, until the last is composed of Air, Fire, Water, Earth, and Spirit, or ∞od, *Heh, Vau, Heh,* and *Shin*, in which the form is visible because of the existence of the spirit. By the cry

"Yehe Aur" (Let there be Light) was the world created, and Yehe is a combination of ∞od and *Heh* (hy) - the Great Father and the Great Mother - the eternal complements.

Finally, it may be asked: What was the reason for the creation? And the Qabalist answers: This is not a rightful question, because God is beyond reason. To him Omnipotence supposes Authority, Necessity, and Liberty, and through Necessity the universe came into being in the form of Authority and Liberty - law and free will. Necessity is in fact the Divine Mystery which is beyond all Reason. It exists; it is, "I Am", the Secret of Elohim.

The Experimental Worlds.

Before the "Spirit of God moved upon the face of the waters" and cast the divine shadow on the formless void, we are told again and again in the *Zohar* that experimental worlds had existed and had been destroyed on account of their imperfection. We read

Before the Aged of the Aged (the Ain Soph), the Concealed of the Concealed, expanded into the form of King, the Crown of Crowns (Kether), there was neither being nor end. He hewed and incised forms and figures into it in the following manner: He spread before him a cover, and carved therein Kings (worlds) and marked out their limits and forms, but they could not preserve themselves. Therefore it is written, "These are the kings that reigned in the land of Edom before there reigned any king over the children of Israel" *(Genesis* xxxvi, 31). This refers to the primordial kings and primordial Israel. All these were imperfect: He therefore removed them and let them vanish, till he finally descended himself to this cover and assumed a form. [5]

But though they vanished they were not annihilated, because "Nothing perisheth in this World, not even the breath which issued from the mouth, for this, like everything else, has its place and destination, and the Holy One, blessed be his Name! turns it into service". [6]

These worlds were formless, "Because the Sacred Aged had not as yet assumed his form", the King and queen as opposite sexes, "and the Master was not yet at his work". [7] By the word "Master" is meant Adam Qadmon, the human form which deity must of necessity assume. It was, therefore, after the destruction of the worlds of the Kings of Edom that the *Latens Deitas* was able to assume a balanced form in the fourth and material world. Thus the *Zohar* says:

The Holy One, blessed be He, created and destroyed several worlds before the present one was made, and when the last work was nigh completion, all the things of this world, all the creatures of the universe, in whatever age they were to exist, before ever they entered into this world, were present before God in their true form. Thus are the words of *Ecclesiastes* to be understood: "What was, shall be and what has been done, shall be done." [8]

This strange story is both obscure and perplexing, because it is difficult to attribute imperfection to God. But to the Qabalist it is otherwise, for the No-Thing evolves into the Some-Thing, the Who; and necessity creeps in, for necessity is impossible without a choice, and choice demands the existence of opposing forces, the male and the female, or the positive and the negative. We are told somewhat mysteriously:

> Before the Forms of the Holy King, the Atteek, were prepared, It built worlds and made Forms for their preservation, but the female principle was not joined yet with the male principle. . . . Therefore they could not exist until this was done. [9]

Until this balance was established Adam Qadmon could not appear and replace the Adam Belial of the unbalanced world and the Averse Tree of Life from which the races of the Gentiles are sprung. It would, therefore, appear that the reason for the creation of the Kings of Edom was to account for the world being peopled with races other than that of Israel.

Adam Qadmon.

On several occasions already have we made mention of Adam Qadmon. He is called by various names, such as the Primordial Man, the Archetypal Man, Microprosopos, the Man of the East, the Shadow of the Invisible Macrocosm, the Pre-existing Soul of Messiah, the Cosmic Son, etc., etc. Strictly speaking, he is the Form, not the Spirit, of Deity in Atziluth. Nevertheless, he is also the emanations of this form in the remaining three worlds; consequently there are four Adam Qadmons.

As regards the first of these Isaac Myer writes

> The Qabbalah shows the existence of four Adams, or rather three continuations of the Upper Heavenly Adam. I. The Perfect Upper Heavenly Adam of the *Atzeel-atic* World, the World of Emanation. It is androgenic and the sole occupant of that world. It is thought of as a manifestation of the Deity in the Divine *D'yook-nah* [shadow], or an undefined phantom shade of the *Tzelem* [image], which the earthly man, in the flesh, has never seen. It is a perfect *Tzure,* or Prototype, to the second and subsequent Adams. In the Upper Heavenly Man is the perfect Holy *Nephesh* [instincts], *Rua'h* [Reason], *Neshamah* [moral consciousness], *'Hayyah* [animal vitality] and *Ye'hee-dah* [personality], merged in combination yet existing *quasi* separately. Here is also the content of the Upper Ten Sephiroth. It answers to the Intellectual, the Brain, and is in the Upper Inner Emanated Heaven. It also answers to the Holy Upper *Neshamah* Soul. [10]

As regards the next three, Myer is more than unreliable, for he is misleading; consequently we will rely on our own interpretation: each is, a shadow or lower appearance of the one above; the second being attributed to the Briatic World, Metatron, and the Rua'h; the third to the Yetziratic World, Sammael, and the Nephesh; the fourth to the Assiatic World, YHVH, and the 'Hayah (or 'Hay-yah) the Supernal Man of *Genesis* i, 26. Together they represent the Grand Personality or Great Universal Man, the synthesis of Adam Qadmon in the four worlds.

In the world of Assiah, Adam Qadmon is the symbolical reflection of God, not on the illuminated void, but on the mist of matter, and by this reflection is the earthly Adam created. He is androgenous like his greater prototype in Atziluth, being both male and female, and therefore he possesses the power to create and to destroy life; that is to exhale it and breathe it in. Thus we see evolved that mysterious and mystical order of revolution. First there is God, or the Gods, energy finding its source in the Ayin. Finally, in the reflection of God is the world emanated, and from the earth emerges man in the form of conscious matter. God in Himself is unity, the world is duality, and man is trinity in unity. And as the Spirit of God moved upon the face of the waters, so does the intelligence of man move upon the face of the fluxes of matter, and through equilibrium it seeks loss of its identity by stilling them in the Spirit of God. When this is accomplished, then will the Magic Mirror of Illusion vanish into the No-Thing-ness out of which it was evolved.

In the account of the creation in *Genesis* the Androgenic Man appears on the sixth day, that is at the end of the creation, because he symbolizes its totality and completion and six is the number of the Great Work; 666 being also its number in the vital, intellectual, and spiritual planes, the *Vau* extended from Malkuth to Kether.

In the second account of the creation the Androgenic Man is formed of the dust of the ground, and the Lord God, that is Tetragrammaton Elohim, and not merely Elohim as in the first account, "breathed into his nostrils the breath of life" (that is the Nephesh), "and man became a living soul". [11] Next the Neshamah (Eden), the garden of the intellect, is planted and man is put into it but is oblivious of the knowledge of good and evil, because as yet he possesses no Rua'h (that is power of judgment), and it is only after the temptation of Eve that the Rua'h is established and the Androgenic Man becomes fully active.

Until this transformation takes place it would appear that the Androgenic Man is only occultly the shadow of Tetragrammaton. He is not YHVH (hvhy) but YVY (yvy); for the *Zohar* informs us "that God brought them [Man shaped for this world and man shaped for the future world] under the aegis of His own name by shaping the two eyes like the letter ∞*od* and the nose between them like the letter *Vau*". [12] At once we see the connection, for YVY equals 26, the numerical value of Tetragrammaton; further, as we will show later on, by splitting one of the two ∞*odin* into *Heh* and *Heh* (10 into 5, 5) and inserting the *Vau* between them we obtain HVH (hvh)-Eve. Again, as already explained, the two ∞*odin* and the *Vau* are the members of the letter *Aleph,* the first letter of the mystical creative alphabet. We are also told in the *Zohar* that when the first man was created, God "gathered the dust from all the four sides of the world . . . and spread upon her a Soul of Life from the holiness Above"; [13] that this

Soul was the Neshamah, which, like the mystery above, comprised three degrees - Nephesh, Rua'h, Neshamah. The third corresponds to the Briatic World, the second to the Yetziratic, and the first to the Assiatic, the body of man being the mystical and magical Merkabah.

It is also to be noted, that the *Neshamah* has three divisions, the highest is the *Ye'hee-dah,* the middle the *'Hay-yah,* the last and third the *Neshamah,* properly to say. They manifest themselves in the *Ma'hshabah* Thought, *Tzelem* Phantom of the Image, *Zurath* Prototypes, and the *D'yooq-nah* Shadow of the phantom Image. The *D'mooth* Likeness or Similitude is a lower manifestation. [14]

Such was the organization of the Great Vitality, the Adam Qadmon of Assiah, who for "a hundred and thirty years had . . . .intercourse with female spirits", [15] begetting the evil powers of the world, powers which are endowed with life but not with immortality until they have been set in conflict with the good and have become equilibrated. To effect this transmutation demanded an angelic race of men and, consequently, the creation of the Angelic Mother.

The Creation of Eve.

In the second chapter of *Genesis* we are told that Tetragrammaton Elohim took a rib from the body of Adam and from it fashioned woman - the passive or feminine essence of the Archetypal Man. The Qabalistic interpretation is as follows: the rib is the letter ∞od, which when removed from the four letters ∞*od Heh Vau Heh* leaves *Heh Vau Heh*, or EVE. The actual transmutation from ∞*od Vau* ∞*od* to ∞*od Heh Vau Heh* we have already described. The ∞*od*, as it will be remembered, also symbolizes the ten Sephiroth of the Yetziratic World, which are reflected in the Assiatic World in the form of the Garden of Eden, which mystically is the Garment of God. The ∞*od* being extracted, the Mystical Eye is closed - that is, the vision of the Yetziratic Tree of Life is cut off from the world of Assiah; consequently, though Adam and Eve perceived that they were naked, they were not ashamed - that is they could not perceive the nakedness of the Assiatic World - because the Yetziratic vision having vanished there was no comparison (duality) left to judge it by. They were in fact bereft of all power of directly perceiving the Shekinah, or Supernal Light.

There is yet another mystery included in the letter ∞*od*. Its hieroglyphic is the human hand. When opened it symbolizes the Microcosm: the four fingers the material elements *(∞od, Heh, Vau, Heh),* and the thumb the spiritual element *(Shin)*. When closed it symbolizes unity, the egg out of which all things emanate. As its numerical value is 10 it also symbolizes the two hands; the erect or good pentagram and the inverted or evil pentagram (see Diagram 4 on page 53). Ten is a combination of unity and zero; therefore mystically there is a relationship between ∞*od* and *Aleph,* and ∞*od* and what is beyond *Aleph* - the beginning. The numerical value of *Aleph* is one, the two arms of which convey the meaning of "as above so beneath". In this letter is symbolized the whole of creation. The top arm is Deity, the cross-bar the waters, motionless as zero, and the lower arm the reflection of the higher arm on the waters. Thus we obtain from a ~, or $1 \div 0 \div 1$, or $10 \div 0 \div 10$; the first equals 2, the second 20, and ∞*od* spelt in full - ∞*od Vau Daleth* - equals 20; therefore the two together equal 22, that is the twenty-two letters of the Hebrew alphabet which constitute the paths of the Tree of Life and out of which, with the Sephiroth, the universe is mystically formed. Finally, as ∞*od* represents the ten Sephiroth and the twenty-two paths, it is the symbol of all things concentrated in the Primordial Point.

In the third chapter of *Genesis* the fall of man is described. To the Qabalist it depicts the first step in the redemption of Tetragrammaton; for unless Eve had tempted Adam, good and evil could never have been harmonized. The apple is the Sephirah of ∞*esod* - the Foundation and the source of generative and regenerative power.

We have described how evil, really activity, emanated out of God in the form of Tetragrammaton. This being so, according to Qabalistic philosophy, out of evil must good, or God, evolve; for "as above so beneath" and "as beneath so above" are the laws of Qabalistic inversion. Just as the Serpent of Kronos devoured its tail, so must evil, in the form of the Satanic Serpent, devour itself This magical operation of activity eating up activity is the central principle in the Messianic act, which we will examine more fully in the next chapter. Here we will restrict ourselves to a few introductory remarks.

Diagram 4: The Good and Evil Pentagrams

The Messianic Redemption.

To begin with there is no Serpent; then one Serpent; lastly two forms of one Serpent, that is a Serpent possessing two complementary energies which when balanced cause its immediate destruction. These two energies, or powers, are called Metatron and Sammael; and in the name of Tetragrammaton they are symbolized by the ∞ *od* and the *Vau - the* Serpent coiled up or passive and the Serpent erect or active. The first represents the creative energy and the second actual movement or change. These two Serpents are the guardians of those forces which man calls good and evil; they are, as we have already mentioned, symbolized by Yakhin and Boaz, the pillars of Solomon's Temple, and flow into Kether through the fifty gates of Binah, 50 being the numerical value of KL (l k) which means "all", or the "understanding of all". Moses failed to open the fiftieth of these gates had he done so he would have become the Messiah of Israel. When the Messiah does come, the Sabbatic Millenary will be accomplished; all Israel will be blessed, [16] and will become one nation in the Lord [17] - that is to say, this world will be inhabited solely by the Chosen People.

There is the energy of the Serpent of *Genesis*, NChSh (Nachash) and the energy of the Brazen Serpent which healed the afflicted Israelites, MShICh (Messiah). Both have the same numerical values, namely 358; consequently when one is subtracted from the other the result is zero - that is deliverance from both good and evil.

In order to understand this we will repeat it again: good is a means of balancing out evil, and evil a means of balancing out good. Neither is desirable in itself except in the Material World, which cannot exist without them; equally, the Spiritual World cannot be entered as long as they exist; consequently their adverseness is purely relative to the Spiritual World. Further on in this book we will show that the power of using either is drawn from the same source - *Shin*, Shekinah, Astral Light, Ether, Electricity, whatever name it may be called by - and to understand the use of this force, yet never to be obsessed by it, is to trample on the head of the Serpent and so re-establish the *Shin* in the body of Tetragrammaton and formulate the Messiah, the Incarnate Word which when disincarnated caused the Assiatic World to be.

In brief, this is the central doctrine of the Qabalistic Redemption; yet so dangerous did this doctrine appear, should it be divulged to the uninitiated, that to safeguard it it was locked away in a jumble of symbols, names, figures, and cryptograms which are frequently contradictory. The danger was that this philosophy not only harmonized good and evil, but maintained that all goodness proceeds from evil. Mystically this means a return of man to God, but by the ignorant it might easily be interpreted as meaning the doing of evil for the sake of spiritual gain.

We will repeat it again: to the Hebrew mystic the God of *Genesis,* Tetragrammaton Elohim, is not the ultimate God, or Ayin, the incomprehensible No-Thing, but Its lowest emanation - matter, or grossness, personified; a reflection of a reflection four times removed. Yet this emanation is the only one which can be comprehended by man, who in this Microcosmic life can only struggle forward through the clash between passivity and activity, which are both good and evil according to circumstances - that is according to necessity. Necessity is Divinity in hiding: Authority is the Divinity of the religious order and Liberty is Divinity in man. The establisher of Authority is the Messiah.

These mystical philosophers fully recognized the necessity for "original sin", because the world is of Satan and man is of the world. Man is born in sin; not the sin of Adam's disobedience, carnal or physical sin, but in the mystical and spiritual sin of Tetragrammaton's fall. The blame was thrown upon Adam, the man, not out of deference to the Deity, but to conceal this potent secret from the uninitiated. In order to redeem the sin in which all mankind is born, it was necessary that a passiveactive emanation be created to balance the active-passive Satanic force. This emanation was to be the Messiah of the world, on whose advent equilibrium would be re-established. This supreme cancellation was the one hope of Israel.

CHAPTER V

THE REDEMPTION OF TETRAGRAMMATON

Symbols of the Messianic Act

As we have shown in the last chapter, the Messianic Act consists of a "transubstantiation" of the material into the spiritual; that is of the Assiatic World into the Yetziratic; in other words, a reversal of the whole process of creation. In the everyday meaning of the words, its object is not to establish law and order, or the happiness of mankind, or to substitute good for evil, but diametrically the opposite: namely to produce anarchy and discontent of so potent a nature that the complementary forces in this world will annihilate one another through the intensity of their friction. To illustrate this by a scientific example: suppose that the universe were composed of the gases oxygen and hydrogen which had been created by electrolysing water; then the Messianic Act would consist in destroying this universe so that it might be replaced by the water out of which it had been formed.

To carry this illustration further: suppose that the four worlds of the Qabalistic cosmology are represented by ice, water, steam, and gas, and that their final state is called electricity, or complete dematerialization (No-Thingness); then the ultimate object of the Messianic Act is to re-establish this Nirvana. Symbolically, this potent mystery is depicted in the eucharist, or high mass, in which the bread and the wine are transmuted into the body and blood of Christ; that is matter into God.

As we have already stated, it was on account of the potency of this mystery that it was so heavily shrouded. Here existed an idea which could either re-create Divinity or plunge mankind into still deeper depths of Devilry. It could exalt man to supreme genius or cast him down into complete madness. Its potency was so stupendous that it may be compared to atomic energy in the physical world; for − "as above so beneath" - it followed that its destructive force was as great as its creative force. Which would be used depended entirely upon the will of the user. Therefore it is the Will which is the redeemer.

Man the Instrument of Redemption.

Though we cannot consciously transcend our reason, we can transcend the realized and gain knowledge of things which we cannot explain or even understand. For instance, we know that the birth of a child must be preceded by union between the opposite sexes; but we cannot explain how this union results in the *creation* of life, or how it is that the child inherits instincts, talents, and defects, or possesses genius, or is born an idiot. Here we are faced by mysteries which lead us deeper and deeper into unconscious realms - that is into realms beyond our reason - and when we enter these realms all we can do is to speak symbolically.

Instead, if we turn from the body to the soul, supposing it to be the Bride of God and God the Bridegroom, we may consciously realize that union has taken place; but when the spiritual child is born we cannot explain the divine process of creation, and the more we attempt to explain it the more obscure become our symbols, every one of which is in fact a lie, that is a misrepresentation of the unconscious or super-conscious to the conscious.

To the Qabalist, as there are two principles in every human being - the active and the passive - because of the law of inversion there must also be two principles within the Divinity. To Him the great work of redemption is not to redeem ourselves, or to be redeemed by the Divine Power, but to redeem Tetragrammaton, the fallen God of the Yetziratic World. The active principle in man must unite with the passive principle in YHVH, and the passive principle in man must submit to union with the active principle in YHVH. From this dual marriage between man and Divinity will emanate the Child, or Messiah, a complete integration of man in God and of God in man.

As through the divine fall the Divinity became manifest in Adam Qadmon, accordingly must man emulate him and through his own transfiguration destroy the material form of consciousness, so that the mirror of illusions may dissolve. Thus will Divinity be redeemed by the destruction of the divine image and the ineffable *Shin* will be reabsorbed into the body of Tetragrammaton. Man must suffer for God - just as in Christian theology, which in so many ways inverts Hebrew theology, Christ must suffer for man, so that God may become the Perfect One. Thus the crucifixion of mankind is the necessary consequent of the divine fall. Man is, therefore, the implement of the redemption of God. This is the secret the Qabalah hints at but never clearly expresses.

The Accomplishment of the Messianic Act.

In the second chapter of *Genesis* Tetragrammaton created Adam Qadmon in his own form. He took "dust of the ground, and breathed into his nostrils the breath of life; and man became a living soul". [1] Next Adam was placed in the Garden of Eden, that is in Malkuth, which is magically divided by four rivers. [2] This means that man, or the humanity of Adam, becomes the *Shin* surrounded by the four elements, or the four magical powers of courage, will, knowledge, and silence. In the centre of the Garden is planted a tree, symbolic of the living force, from the root of which spring three trunks. As already explained in a former chapter, the central one leads to the life supernal and the remaining two include the life infernal; all three, springing from one root, Malkuth, find their unity in Kether. Only by eating of the fruits of the infernal branches and digesting these fruits can Adam compel the central trunk to grow, and only when its topmost branches are climbed will Adam realize the nonexistence of good and evil, and discover the World of Spirit and clothe himself in immortality.

The relationship between Tetragrammaton and humanity the flesh cells, so to speak, of Adam Qadmon - creates the potentialities of Satan (the demon hordes); and as Tetragrammaton is possessed of a horror (a void) when he contemplates the loss of his identity, in order to maintain it secret he forbids Adam to eat of the Tree of Knowledge of Good and Evil, because its fruits are death, that is they lead to passivity - the magical recoil which threatens the active existence of Satan.

Next Eve, the female counterpart of Adam, is formed, and though mystically the man and the woman are created in one form, face to face, allegorically the creation of Eve precedes that of Adam, for allegorically the positive forces of life (the masculine) emanate from the negative forces (the feminine).

By separating the ∞od from Tetragrammaton - (Y)HVH-and thus creating Eve, a stupendous active and consequently demoniacal force is released; for Eve is "the mother of all living things" (including the "Mother of God") the female, or negative, force of Jah (YH) - the *Heh* of which is ever seeking to reunite with the ∞od.

In its lower aspect ∞od represents Microcosmic man; in its higher it represents the Tree of Life and the Tree of the Knowledge of Good and Evil. As man is a trinity in unity inhibited by a gleam of the supernal *Shin* - the *Shin* which, volatilizing into Light, enabled Tetragrammaton to become visible-so also is the ∞od threefold in nature. It represents not only the Pillars of Severity, Mercy, and Mildness, but also formation, reformation, and transformation; activity, passivity, and equilibrium; and good, evil, and deliverance. Thus it is not one ∞od but three $\infty odin$, which to unite must climb the three trunks of the inseparable Trees and, interlacing in Kether, the Crown, reformulate the letter *Shin*, *a* trinity in unity. Thus will it deliver back to Tetragrammaton the power he lost in his fall from the world of Yetzirah. Such is the accomplishment of the Messianic Act.

The Integration of the Disintegrated.

Thus far the mystery of the ∞od, the positive force of Jah (YH); next, as to Eve, who being possessed of the negative force, the *Heh*, has upset the balance of equilibrium.

In the centre of the name of Eve is the active and virile *Vau*, the subtle Serpent of the third chapter of *Genesis*. It is the positive quality of the Messianic Force and is, consequently, an evil which creates good. When we look at the position of this letter and remember the significance of those on its right and left, we at once notice how abnormal its place is. On the left is its natural partner, the first *Heh* or Daughter, its wedded wife; on the right is its Mother, now widowed, because she is separated from the ∞*od* and yet forced into an unnatural union with her Son. She is ever striving to reunite with the ∞*od*, and consequently Eve is tempted to eat of the fruit of the Tree of the Knowledge of Good and Evil. "For God doth know that the day ye eat thereof, then your eyes shall be opened; and ye shall be as gods, knowing good and evil." [3]

The passive forces, symbolized by woman, listen to the lamentation of the primal *Heh,* and then seeing that it was a "Tree to be desired to make one wise" (that is leading from the fiftieth gate of the feminine Binah to the masculine 'Hokmah), Eve plucked of its fruit and handed it to Adam - the active forces. At once the eyes of both "were opened", and they knew that they were naked, that is that an Abyss separated the Supernal Triad from the Infernal Heptad. Thus they became conscious of the difference between YH and VH, and in this consciousness was reflected the unity of these two (Satan) as symbolized by their nakedness.

As the Egyptian hierophants, when they discovered that the earth gravitated round the sun, hid away this knowledge because it revealed the law of attraction and repulsion (the law of creation), so now did man and woman veil the knowledge of the conjunction of the *Vau* and the *Heh* (which is but a reflection of the union of the ∞*od* and the *Heh)* by means of aprons, tha:t is by turning this knowledge into a mystery

No sooner were the mysteries hidden than the eternal opposites, the man and the woman, heard the voice of Tetragrammaton "walking in the garden". It is the Primal Light, *Shin,* formulated by the mystic union of the ∞*od* and *Heh* (Jah) and the *Vau* and *Heh* (Veh). As they heard it they hid themselves from "the presence of the Lord God". When questioned, the active force *(Vau)* accuses the passive force *(Heh),* and Jah curses the Serpent (the Messianic Force) [4] and assumes his full Satanic form by putting enmity into the heart of woman and sorrow into the life of man.

Then he clothes them in animal desires which are symbolized by the coats of skins. That this is the voice of the fallen Sammael of Yetzirah there can be no doubt, because Tetragrammaton says to Eve: "Thy desire shall be to thy husband, and he shall rule over thee" ; [5] in other words - the passive shall be subservient to the active, which means that equilibrium cannot be established. Lastly, Tetragrammaton acknowledges the active force by saying:

Behold, the man is become as one of us [the *Elohim*], to know good and evil; and now, lest he put forth his hand, and take also of the tree of life, and eat, and live for ever: Therefore the Lord God sent him forth from the Garden of Eden, to till the ground from whence he was taken. So he drove out the man; and he placed at the east of the garden of Eden, cherubims, and a flaming sword which turned every way, to keep the way of the tree of life. [6]

Herein is hidden a profound mystery: the man *alone* is cast out of Eden, but not so the woman - the final *Heh* remains in the Garden of Mystery; the *Vau* is cast outside. This separation at once disintegrates Tetragrammaton: the ∞*od* becomes the Tree of Life; the primal *Heh,* the Tree of the Knowledge of Good and Evil; the Kerubim, the material aspects of ∞*od, Heh, Vau, Heh;* and the flaming sword, the *Shin.* Thus Tetragrammaton is disintegrated and there is separation everywhere. As with Osiris, the Great Work now consists in reuniting the fragments; the *Vau,* or creative phallus, being cast out of the Garden into the World. The *Vau* must unite with the *Heh,* for when it does so, in accordance with the magical law of inversion (Necessity), the ∞*od* will unite with the *Heh,* and the *Shin - the* Flaming Sword (see Diagram 3, page 34) - will be plunged into the heart of Tetragrammaton. Then will the Kerub of Earth, [7] which is the unity of the forces of the remaining three Kerubim, be sacrificed - that is materiality will vanish; the Trees of Life and of Good and Evil will dissolve into one; and as this unity takes form, not only will Tetragrammaton be re-established, but simultaneously will he become ∞*od Heh Shin Vau Heh* (hvwhy), [8] the Messiah. Then will the world of Assiah vanish into the ecstasy of Yetzirah; matter will have become pure form - that is a mathematical conception, a thought.

The Creation of Hell.

Though the world of Assiah is ruled by the inverse Sammael (Tetragrammaton despiritualized), and is, consequently, the realm of demoniacal forces, it is not Hell as conceived by the Qabalist, for Hell is the reflection, or shadow, of this world; that is the abode of active forces turned upside down, the chaos which has to be stilled in order that *Shin*, the Shikinah, [9] or Divine Majesty, can be perfectly reflected.

With the disintegration of Tetragrammaton we sink into the carnal, or mundane, aspect of the mystery, the immediate consequences of this disruption being the birth of Love and Power, which before were united in a close embrace. The first is the feminine, or passive, quality in humankind, the Venus force; and the second the active and masculine quality, the Mars force. Mystically their separation is evil, because it causes striving to reunite; but humanly these qualities are not wicked in themselves, though they may become sinful, for out of love can emerge lust and hatred, and out of power fear and cruelty. The demoniac can consequently become the diabolic.

The disruption of Tetragrammaton, which is necessary for the redemption of Tetragrammaton, is followed by the story of Cain and Abel, [10] the conflict between power and love. The Venusian and Martian forces in life are divided against each other, life being the synthesis of these two; and the mystical quality of evil emanates as common mundane wickedness, which leads to murder - the destruction of life - not its transformation.

Later on this wickedness is followed by the magical prostitution of evil, or the act of Magical Incest, through the intermingling of the Sons of God (the demoniac powers engendered by the disruption of Tetragrammaton) with the daughters of men[11] - the carnal lusts of humankind. Here is symbolized a process of levelling down (a carnal communism) and not of rising up, and the result is the establishment of Black Magic, the earth being peopled by "mighty men", [12] or despots. Why not White Magic? Because the Sons of God (the Above) came *down* to the daughters of men (the Below); that is light is absorbed by darkness.

Thus mankind sank into the Qliphoth, the reflection of the world of Assiah upon the chaos of human passions, and Hell is created - the materialized mental pit. Thus also it came about that the world became corrupt and filled with violence, and to redeem it it was necessary to destroy it, except for Noah and those in the Ark. Noah was, however, far from perfect; consequently we find that after the deluge he profanes the Mysteries, "And he drank of the wine, and was drunken; and he was uncovered within his tent" [13] and, his son Canaan divulging this profanation, is cursed. Thus magic, in spite of the repentance of Tetragrammaton, continued to grow until the repopulated world cried:

"Go to, let us build us a city, and a tower whose top may reach unto heaven; and let us make us a name," [14] that is an object of worship; [15] for they had a crafty design to rid themselves of the Supreme Power and to transfer His glory to another. [16]

The inner meaning of the Tower of Babel is that any attempt to possess the secrets of heaven in order to divulge them to the uninitiated on earth must lead to misunderstanding and anarchy - a confusion of tongues, that is of false symbols. A universal pentacle cannot be constructed for the unpurified multitudes, for the multitudes can only comprehend parables.

We have now descended a long way in the hierarchy of evil. From the divine we have touched bottom in the magical, and yet all we have explained is included in the words of the Emerald Tablet of Hermes Trismegistus:

"That which is above is like that which is below, and that which is below is like that which is above, for the operations of the wonders of the one thing." "To deny hell", writes Éliphas Lévi, "is also to deny heaven" then he says:

Seeing that, according to the most exalted interpretation of the Great Hermetic Dogma, hell is the equilibrating reason of heaven, for harmony results from the analogy of contraries, *Quod superius, sicut quod inferius.* Superiority presupposes inferiority; the depth determines the height, and to fill up the valleys is to efface mountains, so also to take away shadows would be to destroy light, as this is only visible by the graduated contrast of darkness and day; a universal obscurity would be produced by all-dazzling brilliance. The very existence of colour in light is due to the presence of shadow; it is the triple alliance of day and night, the luminous image of dogma, the light made shadow, and the Saviour is the Word made man. All this rests on the same law, which is the first law of creation, the one absolute law of Nature, being that of distinction and harmonious balancing of opposing forces in universal equilibrium. [17]

The Source of Messianic Power.

As the creation of the world was out of chaos, so must its destruction, which carries with it its spiritual resurrection, be through chaos; such is the simple logic of the Qabalah.

As God is the consciousness of the Macrocosm, so is man the consciousness of the Microcosm; such is the simple mystery of the Qabalah. In the human world man is a god knowing good and evil, yet he is also the son of the God of the natural world - the creator of good and evil. As consciousness has been precipitated from the source of all things, so is it man's lot to expand his atom of consciousness until it fills eternity and merges once again into the source from whence it emanated. Little by little in this upward evolution are all things intellectualized and in consequence destroyed. Thus the unknown becomes the known and ceases to exist because its knowability is death to its mystery; that is to say it is bereft of opposition to the consciousness of man. Thus the search for knowledge is an unending campaign against duality in which conquest deprives the conquered of its activity, its opposition, which in man is shadowed forth as ignorance. A void is created, and over it the Spirit (Shekinah) in man moves and respiritualizes the gross incarnation of Tetragrammaton and so formulates the Messiah.

The laboratory of the Devil (Satan of the Qliphoth) is the heart of man; herein are all things human conceived and ordered.

Mystically this heart is the Ark which rode out the terrors of the flood, just as the *Shin* rode out the terrors of the darkness which "was upon the face of the deep". The timber it is built of is cut from the branches of the Tree of Life. In it is carried the cubic Stone of the Wise, the Corner Stone of the Qabalistic Temple (the divine form of Adam Qadmon), the apex of which is the letter ∞*od*, and at the corners of whose triangular base stand the letters *Heh, Vau, Heh*, and in whose centre, unseen from outside, is the letter *Shin*. This letter, as we have already explained, symbolizes among other things the crucifixion of Christ - Christ between the aggressive and passive thieves. As Christ expires, His soul is liberated and the veil of the Temple (the pyramid) is rent in the midst. The three flames, or

∞*odin*, of the letter *Shin* represent the Od, Aur, and Ob, the active, equilibrating, and passive forces of life – a trinity in unity. The Messianic Act, or Great Work, consists in freeing the hidden *Shin* from the elemental pyramid in which it is imprisoned. Then the four elements vanish and the splendour of the Shekinah enwraps, like a caul of light, the Divine Child - the Messiah.

From this esoteric doctrine it will be seen that the Messiah does not come from outside, he does not descend upon the pyramid; in place he comes from inside and dissolves the pyramid. The Christian idea of the Son of God descending from heaven to save the world is in fact the Qabalistic idea upside down; for all men, or, according to the Hebrews, all the Chosen People, are sons of God, particles of divinity, atoms of spirit, and when all these atoms unite in one spiritual ecstasy the Messiah is born; for he is the integration of the totality of spirit in mankind. Not a spark descending into darkness, but darkness dissolving into illimitable light. From the active to the formal, from the formal to the creative, from the creative to the archetypal, and thence back into the No-Thingness, the source and the end of all things: such is the complete Messianic hypostasis.

CHAPTER VI

THE SOURCE OF MYSTIC POWER

The Essence of the Qabalah.

THE Wisdom of the Qabalah may be sublime or it may be diabolical; but whatever its values are, one thing is certain: they are utterly confused. The *Zohar*, our main source of Qabalistic knowledge, is like an untidy pawn-shop - a jumble of trash and articles of value. Here are crowded together and stacked up the cast-off intellectual clothing of many minds, cheap jewellery, base metals thinly plated, gold, silver, copper, and brass. Yet if we delve deep enough among the rubbish which encumbers its shelves, we shall, as we have shown we can, now and again find a pearl of great price.

The supernal diadem is there, but it has been broken up, the urge of secrecy having dismembered it and hidden its priceless fragments away in the most unlikely and inacessible corners. This secrecy has all but defeated its own end by so obscuring truth that in many cases it is no longer discoverable. And when by much searching and labour we do find some precious stone, symbolism has cut it into so many facets that it is all but impossible to judge of its true shape. We look at it from one side and see one thing, then from another and see another, the very brilliance of the symbols confusing us.

In Chapters I to V we have attempted - and acknowledgedly with but limited success - to project a beam of light into the chaotic lumberrooms of Zoharic learning and illumine what therein lies stored. Nevertheless, we believe that the little we have discovered is of priceless value, because also do we believe much of it to be universally true, offering to the tumultuous years in which we live a key to the door which at present bars us from a completer understanding.

Today we wait on the threshold of this door, fearfully gazing out upon a world monstrous and twoheaded. Darkness has taken upon itself a political form which has bereft the nations of their sight; has shrouded their minds and blotted out their wisdom; has sown among them the dragon's teeth of war. We stand today at the foot of the Tower of Babel - the tower of class strife and international conflict.

Meanwhile light has scintillated forth in science, the boundless Shekinah of this present age. It is girt by no frontier and circumscribed by no class. It shines forth over the north and the south, over the east and the west. Into the heights and into the depths it glows, and yet for the perfection of its creative force it demands that upon its ever-expanding effulgence be cast the shadow of a new human form: the shadow of a humanity in which the physical, the moral, and the intellectual are balanced between the material and the spiritual. What the world demands is a new Microcosmic Idea, a new five-fold Messianic Force, a new Dispensation of Balance which will establish within it a new equilibrium.

As science is a universal understanding of things, and as the Qabalah purports to be the key to universal wisdom, then, if this wisdom fits this understanding, will this key unlock the door before which we blindly stand. What then is there common between science and the Qabalah? Before answering this question we will attempt to reduce much of what we have as yet tried to explain to its simplest form.

(1)   Man is a mystery shrouded in a mystery which we call the universe; and this mystery leads us to a yet deeper mystery which we call God or the Unknowable. All is a three-fold wonder, a relationship between God, man, and the universe.

(2)   This universe comes from some unknown source and wends its way towards some unknown end. As it comes from -?, appears to be proceeding towards -?, and is in itself -?, its nature, form, and powers can only be described by means of symbols; that is in pictures which in themselves are no more real than a photograph is real when compared to the thing it represents.

(3)   As symbols are but thoughts set forth in pictorial form which possess no activity, we conclude that the world in which we live, and which in fact is shadowed forth by our thoughts, is no more than one infinite thoughtform, a form which exists (how is beyond our understanding) in God, or the Unknowable, and which finds its activity in our thoughts by being fragmented by our finite minds.

(4)   To us our thought would be impossible without light, and light would be incomprehensible without darkness, just as heat is incomprehensible without cold. To us, in its ultimate form, the universe is light; it is that which opens the mind of the thinker, which, however, cannot comprehend the existence of light without lack of light.

(5)   This light reveals to us a universe of four dimensions, of four worlds in one manifestation, of space and of time the former being built up of three directions, length, breadth, and thickness. The one encloses or includes the other, and what is beyond this four-dimensional universe is unknown, if not unknowable.

6) In its turn darkness reveals to us the limitations of human knowledge. Our minds may be compared to fire-flies flitting about in the cavern of night. The minute glow which they emit and cast on the void not only shows us how vast is our ignorance, but that all our knowledge can be no more than relatively true, for the mind is finite and the cavern apparently infinite.

(7)   As all knowledge can be no more than relatively true - that is never free from ignorance - wisdom consists in recognizing this fact and of utilizing knowledge in accordance with circumstances. Understand the circumstances and through knowledge extract light (higher Knowledge) from them - this is wisdom; but to use knowledge in order to extract power (the clash between light and darkness) - this is magic.

(8)   Wherever we turn we come up against a three-fold order: within man in the form of the physical, moral, and intellectual spheres of his activities between men in that of justice, culture, and work: between man and the universe and between man and God - between everything. Nothing in this world is single; not even a thought is single. All things and all thoughts are relative; that is, they are the offspring of a relationship, of an above and of a below.

(9)   Relativity is, consequently, the secret of deliverance from darkness; therefore it is the road towards the expansion of light. And as light grows, so does thought grow. Consequently, when light has reached its utmost limits, thought will do likewise, and the one Thought-Form will be re-created. This we feel is the ultimate end of the human will - the myriads of fragments of thought reestablished in the Primal Idea.

(10)   Finally, this transfiguration can only be accomplished through action, that is through will to think or to stop thinking. The world we live in is a world of activity, a conflict between light and darkness, knowledge and ignorance, good and evil. It is a whirling energy - nebular force, stellar force, planetary force, human force. It is a world of perpetual revolutions - a cosmos, a chaos, a void, the spark of a new thought; and then once again a cosmos, a chaos, and a void, the shadow of a dead thought. Nature abhors a vacuum; hence life is the plenitude which fills it, a plenitude which of necessity can never stand still. Each true thought; a thought full of light, which flashes on the darkness which surrounds it, is a Christ unto this world. When three such thoughts, one in the physical realm, one in the moral, and one in the intellectual, simultaneously flash forth, then is a Messianic Age begotten. It is this three-fold deliverance which the world awaits - a deliverance and transfiguration which can only come from within.

Such in brief are some of the main doctrines of the Qabalah reduced to their simplest terms and translated into easily understandable language. From them we will turn to the scientific conceptions of today and will show that between these two systems of thought there are certain similarities.

The Mysticism of Modern Science.

The science of today represents, in more than one way, what the scientist of fifty years ago would have called chaos. The law of causation is to disappear, conservation of energy is to disappear, uniformity is to disappear, determinism is to be replaced by probabilities, and Law by Chance. The Law of the rationalists of the nineteenth century was at least something which the mind of man could grip on to; it symbolized order, if not love: but Chance symbolizes neither. To the common mind Chance is something blind, an eyeless force, a kind of omnipotent Cyclops aimlessly tumbling through time and space, to whom the harmony of the spheres means nothing; a sightless gambler who shuffles the lives of men and casts them upon the table of fate, not to play with, but merely to pick them up again and reshuffle the pack.

Surely man himself is within himself superior to this, the latest symbolic emanation of truth. The old struggle with the rationalist conception of the world was how to find a place for freedom in a world where all things were determined by law. The new struggle with the mathematicians would appear to be how to find a place for authority and order in a world of pure chance or pure accident - that is of complete freedom. The one series of symbols led us to a mechanistic world conception - the world as a vast machine; the other leads us to one which can best be compared to a dice-box - accident, luck, odds on or against. In both, however, the Exalted Engineer and the Supreme Gambler remain unexplained; hence there is hope that the present symbols are not final ones, but those only which appeal to a small priesthood as exclusive as the priests of ancient Elusis.

Are these scientific speculations nothing more than symbols? Yes: as to this there can be no doubt. They are not Truth, for at most they are but the reflections of Truth upon the mind of a mathematician - just as the symbols of the first chapter of *Genesis* were the reflections of Truth upon the mind of some early poet, living not in a mathematical civilization, but in a pastoral one. Sir James Jeans, who has done so much to popularize the hidden meanings of present-day science, openly acknowledges this. He tells us that, whilst formerly the scientist looked upon the world as a collection of "hard bits", today he looks upon it as a collection of "electrical waves." These are, he says, of two kinds - "bottled-up waves, which we call matter, and unbottled waves, which we call radiation of light".[1] These waves only exist in our minds, for they are nothing more than mental pictures of a Reality which exists outside the mind - that is beyond the power of thought. Their existence is so completely nebulous that, as Sir James Jeans says, "The making of models or pictures to explain mathematical formulae and the phenomena they describe, is not a step towards, but a step away from, reality; it is like making graven images of a spirit".[2] In fact they cannot be named as tangible things are named, cat - "cat", table - ' 'table", etc., etc., but merely numbered in a symbolical way as mathematical or - to all intents and purposes - as metaphysical quantities.

In that fascinating book *The Mysterious Universe*, Professor Jeans writes

If annihilation of matter occurs, the process is merely that of unbottling imprisoned wave energy, and setting it free to travel through space. These concepts reduce the whole universe to a world of light, potential or existent, so that the whole story of its creation can be told with perfect accuracy and completeness in the six words "God said, Let there be light."[3]

Here, mysteriously, perhaps inevitably, the latest symbols of the creation of the universe in which we live harmonize with those which flashed upon the mind of man thousands of years ago.

What has caused this extraordinary change between the scientific outlook of the present century and that of the last? The answer is largely to be discovered in the Theory of Relativity, which is but another name for the Three-fold Conception - the relationship between two facts as it appears in their resultant.

For instance, the resultant of pressure and resistance is the only means at our disposal of understanding pressure and resistance: if there is no resultant, then pressure and resistance are nonexistent to us.

Formerly this globe of ours was considered to be part of a three-dimensional universe, or space, floating through time. Now time has been added to it as the fourth dimension, and the volume thus conceived is described as a "continuum". The relationship is therefore no longer that of ourselves and space in time, but that of ourselves and the continuum in which time is an integral factor. Today man is no longer faced as he was a couple of centuries ago by a universe of four elements, but instead by a universe of four dimensions - ∞*od, Heh, Vau, Heh,* in a more all-embracing form - which with himself complete the modern idea of the Microcosm.

To Sir James Jeans, in spite of the fact, as he says, that "We have no language at our command except that derived from our terrestrial concepts and experiences", scientific speculations lead to the supposition that "the universe appears to have been designed by a pure mathematician" [4] - a Qabalistic assumption. And what does this mean?

It means that science, which during the last century broke away from the idealistic conceptions of religion - the spiritual side of man - is today tending towards a return to these concepts; for, as this scientist says:

We may think of the electrons as objects of thought, and time as the process of thinking . . . the universe can be best pictured, though still very imperfectly and inadequately, as consisting of pure thought. [5]

Here we return to an idealism which would have staggered the imagination of most of the scientists of half a century ago; but which will be readily accepted by every Qabalist, and would have been accepted by such as a supreme truth even two thousand years ago. And outside the Qabalah this idealism logically brings us back to Bishop Berkeley, the greatest of the idealistic philosophers since Plato. Over two hundred years ago he wrote:

All the choir of heaven and furniture of earth, in a word all those bodies which compose the mighty frame of the world, have not any substance without mind. . . . . . . So long as they are not actually perceived by me, or do not exist in my mind, or in that of any other created spirit, they must either have no existence at all, or else subsist in the mind of some Eternal Spirit [the Ayin].

Quoting these remarkable words of this most remarkable philosopher, Sir James says:

.Modern science seems to me to lead, by a very different road, to a not altogether dissimilar conclusion. Because of our different line of approach we have reached the last of the above three alternatives first, and the others appear unimportant in comparison. It does not matter whether objects "exist in my mind, or in that of any other created spirit" or not; their objectivity arises from their subsisting "in the mind of some Eternal Spirit". [6]

This Eternal Spirit, being the "organ" of creative thought, must be something superior to, or certainly other than, the continuum or four-dimensional universe in which we live; for this continuum exists only in his thought, just as we are in ourselves Superior to our own thoughts, for we are the creators of them and live in the shadow-world created by them. This Spirit must be something which may be called Reality, or Truth (the Macrocosm or Macroprosopos) concerning which the human reason can only form symbolical pictures, reflections in a mirror.

We will attempt to explain this in a simpler way: supposing we could not raise our heads and look at the sun, we could nevertheless examine it indirectly by gazing into a looking-glass placed at our feet. In it we should see a reflection of the sun, the only solar reality possible to us in the circumstances; but it would not be the reality of the sun itself, any more than our image in a mirror is ourself - in fact such an image is in a way upside down, as our right side becomes our left and vice versa. As long as we kept our eyes fixed on the looking-glass, though we should know something about the sun, we should in fact know very little. At times its image would appear and at times vanish, according to the motion of the earth, the state of the atmosphere, or on account of an eclipse. So erratically would its image come and go that we might well say that its movements were directed by chance. Yet if we could only raise our eyes, we should soon discover the reasons why all this was so. The fact is, as Sir James Jeans says:

> Many would hold that, from the broad philosophical standpoint, the outstanding achievement of twentiethcentury physics is not the theory of relativity with its welding together of space and time, or the theory of quanta with its present apparent negation of the laws of causation, or the dissection of the atom with the resultant discovery that things are not what they seem; it is the general recognition that we are not yet in contact with ultimate reality. To speak in terms of Plato's well-known simile, we are still imprisoned in our cave with our backs to the light, and can only watch the shadows on the wall. At present the only task immediately before science is to study these shadows, to classify them and explain them in the simplest possible way. [7]

Scientists are, therefore, concerned in explaining the *shadows* of Reality in terms of the rational symbols of today, just as the Qabalists were concerned in explaining them in terms of the rational (then theological and non-scientific) symbols of their day. Like the Qabalist the scientist can lead us up to the threshold of the symbolic temple of God - this world and universe defined and explained by science (knowledge) – but on account of the limitations of the instrument he uses, namely rational thought, he cannot lead us into it. To enter it we need something, a faculty, which transcends the reason. In the example we have above given of examining the sun by means of a looking-glass because we are unable to raise our heads, this inability may be compared to rational thought, and the raising of our heads to that higher faculty which will enable us to open, as it were, spiritual eyes, and see not only the shadows of Reality but Reality itself.

Since the beginning of written history very little progress has been made in the intellectual interpretation of the mysteries, which stood shrouded before the academies of Aristotle and Plato. Many things have changed, innumerable experiments have been made, yet before the essential mysteries we still stand as blindly as they did. All that has in reality happened is that we have changed our forms of thought; then they were flatter, now they are rounder.

Each new philosophy opens like a fairy-tale, for man is ever, and of necessity must be, a wondering child. There is a man or a woman and a wishing-ring – an unannihilatable atom of magic. The ring is turned and man sees something which does not exist, but which is so remarkable that he persists that it does exist – he is for ever creating the hollow worlds of the Kings of Edom. Today we laugh at Qabalistic learning – why? Because it is out of place and out of time. Tomorrow we shall laugh at the scientific theories of today and for similar reasons. If the universe is really fourdimensional, and certainly it appears to be so, then we are living not on a sphere but on the skin of a hypersphere which we can only explain by means of mathematical symbols. What is a^4? We cannot even draw a picture of it!

Yet we are told, by those we cannot contradict, that "Einstein's universe contains matter but no motion and de Sitter's contain motion but no matter" [8] – on one side "motionless matter" and on the other "matterless motion" – yet that Einstein's universe will end in de Sitter's and de Sitter' in what amounts to zero. [9] Here surely, we are not very distant from the Qabalah, because "undifferentiated sameness" and "nothingness" [10] coincide. Examine the following exposition:

> To the pure geometer the radius of curvature [of spacetime] is an incidental characteristic – like the grin of the Cheshire cat. To the physicist it is an indispensable characteristic. It would be going too far to say that to the physicist the cat is merely incidental to the grin. Physics is concerned with interrelatedness such as the interrelatedness of cats and grins. In this case the "cat without a grin" and the "grin without a cat" are equally set aside as purely mathematical phantasies. [11]

In a spherical universe, if you gaze in any direction long enough – that is if you gaze for six thousand million years – you will see the back of your head. [12] But fortunately we are spared this experiment because a 'perfectly spherical world is a mathematical invention". [13] So also do we conclude are all other worlds fashioned out of thought-forms, whether mathematical religious or whatnot in shape. They are all shadows, all in "substance" illusionary.

Pope said in his *Dunciad*, See Mystery to Mathematics fly!" . . . Still the keystone is mystery. To the Qabalist the number 137 is a number of awe, a complete book of mysteries (Qabalah hlbq = 5 + 30 + 2 +100 = 137). From the Ayin Soph to the three supernal Sephiroth and thence to the seven inferior spheres it symbolizes the entire universe; but to the astronomer it is the value of "the finestructure constant". [14] Something very different, nevertheless something equally mysterious. Yet to scoff at science would be foolishness, just as it is foolishness to scoff at any honest idea. Science is a means to an end - the knowledge of shadows. So also is the qabalah, though it looks at the mystery from a different angle of thought. When the Qabalist says, "As above so beneath", and when the scientist says, "To measure the mass of an electron, a suitable procedure is to make astronomical observations of the distances and velocities of spiral nebulae", [15] these angles all but coincide. And when the Qabalist postulates No-Thingness as the beginning of Every-Thingness, and the scientist says, "The beginning seems to present insuperable difficulties unless we agree to look on it as frankly supernatural", [16] coincidence is absolute; for in both Reality remains impenetrable, and like Bottom's dream all that is derived from this Supreme Zero is without bottom - it is the pit of activities which the Qabalists frequently call hell.

The Laboratory of Satan.

In the world we see a ceaseless struggle entailing change - birth, formation, growth, decay, and death. A ceaseless evolution and dissolution surround us in which everything seems to be possessed of a dual nature and to be urged onwards or backwards by a clash of dual powers. Thus far the duality which lies at the foundation of Qabalistic philosophy appears rational enough. Yet reason cannot tell us whether this duality is the ultimate end, or whether it emanates from unity or from nothingness. Reason is a wonderful ladder which enables us to climb towards the ceiling of the intellectual world, but it does not enable us to penetrate it and to see beyond. This ceiling and all which is contained beneath it belong to the realm of science, which arranges and rearranges the furniture from time to time. Beyond and above is another room - the super-scientific, the super-rational, perhaps a "space" which is no conceivable room at all.

Man, however, has never been content with purely rational answers, for he is possessed by what may be called a "spiritual discontent" which is unsatisfied with all scientific arguments, and which has been both an assistant and resistant to scientific growth. The rationalist says that "the answer to $a + b$ is x; the theologian says "no, it is y"; and between the beliefs and disbeliefs of both has the intellectual world expanded from out of wonders to what we call facts. Yet, however firmly these facts may be founded upon reason, there remains always a doubt. Within the circumference of this doubt lie all religious systems, and its centre, where all doubt ends, is called God.

To a highly intellectual and speculative mind God is a mystery subject only to symbolic explanation; but to the crude, sensuous masses of mankind He and His symbols are one. To the first He is a metaphysical ideal; to the second - a physical fact. As from the Qabalistic mind is evolved an androgenous being whose very existence depends upon the balance of passive and active forces, similarly from the primitive mind of the masses is evolved an anthropomorphic deity who can accomplish good and evil, and who consequently is to be loved and feared. As the mystical Adam Qadmon is the measure of the one, so is the physical Adam, that is man himself, the measure of the other. As the one is explained by symbols, the other is asserted in words. Between the mystical and the superstitious there is consequently a close relationship; and as man, whether mystical or superstitious, lives in one and the same world, both see God in Nature but from different intellectual angles.

The religion of the masses has never changed in essence; for it has always been Nature-worship in one form or another. Life eternal is but a prolongation of life terrestrial; the soul, of the personality; heaven is but a super-happy home and hell but an infra-abominable gaol. Everywhere and in every land we find the same ideas dressed in different garments the same gods and goddesses of chaos and order, of love and death, of hatred and life, of fertility, of dawn, of night, etc., etc. From such is built up the normal religious mood of the masses; nevertheless there is yet another mood, for from time to time in the world's history something happens: a man appears, be he prince or pauper, who throws the masses into such a state of religious fervour that all reason and with it all doubt is obliterated and a spiritual condition is produced which closely resembles physical drunkenness. Such men were Orpheus, Oedipus, Osiris, Zoroaster, Krishna, Odin, Buddha, Christ, Mahomet, and a host of lesser names, mythological and historical, many of which have passed into oblivion. For a time these men have lifted the multitudes out of Nature, endowing them with a spiritual instinct, a Ketheric Nephesh, more powerful than all their natural instincts combined. Self-preservation, self-sacrifice, self-assertion, pugnacity, love, hate, fear, greed, and all the other instincts in man in an instant become slaves to this tyrant. The people are in fact filled with a god, for what the Master says is the voice of the Deity. Yet his words cannot explain his illuminating vision; for all they can do is to translate the super-rational into the rational, that is to render comprehensible the incomprehensible form which he himself can grasp only symbolically. These words are drawn from his sentiments (Nephesh) and his intellect (Rua'h) and not from his spirit (Neshamah); and should his sentiments be gross and his intellect crude, then will his symbols be gross and crude and so will be the words whereby he attempts to explain them.

This brings us back to the opening words of this chapter: it does not matter what an intellectual man or woman may think of the wisdom of the Qabalah; he or she may say, "Well, if these people like to symbolize God as a Satanic force, let them; it is their business and not mine." This is tolerant enough, but it avoids the danger without removing it; which is that should a Qabalist attain to so potent a vision that he can detonate the spiritual instinct of the masses, will he not, because of his education, make use of a Satanic symbology which, literally accepted by his intoxicated followers, will spiritually turn them upside down and impel them towards the most diabolical acts of anarchy and outrage?

The likelihood of this is common knowledge, for the power of the demagogue is well known, and the most dangerous of demagogues is he who is fervently narrow in his opinions or faith, that is single-minded. How much more, then, is he who believes that his voice is God's voice, the veritable Logos, God being symbolized to him according to what his sentiments, intellect, and education make him, and God to his listeners being fashioned according to their level of intelligence! If the symbols are accepted as realities by his followers, and if his darkness, lit by his spiritual frenzy, finds a sympathetic and passive partner in their ignorance and animality (the chaos of his would-be cosmos), then the child of this union will not be Lucifer, the intellectual Satan, but Belial, his sensuous or Qliphothic counterpart. Then will the surroundings of his followers be turned into a physical hell.

It was for this reason that the Qabalists locked away their secrets from the uninitiated, and that every other truly religious cult has done the same; for the Spirit of God cannot be reflected upon chaos except as a broken, jagged, and turbulent star of light which maddens its watchers in place of illumining them.

This, we are of opinion, will be accepted by most thinkers, though many will refuse to differentiate between the demagogue and the religious master, because the power of both these soul-troublers varies in degree. This is so, yet this variance opens up an important problem: namely, why does it vary? We know that in the material world conviction depends on one or more of the three spheres of power - the physical, sensuous, and the intellectual - and that this mastership stands beyond good and evil because it is a power for good and evil. A skilled craftsman may use his energy and talents for the benefit or detriment of mankind, and so also a skilled demagogue or a skilled philosopher. Is not a similar process also applicable to the spiritual sphere, granted that there is such a sphere? And if this be not granted, then some abnormal intellectual or sensuous sphere must be assumed. To us the threefold order is not alone patent to the Qabalah, but is an obvious rational conception. We know that we are composed of matter, but matter plus something we call our ego. We know that we are living matter, and that the earth we come from is not living matter in the sense that we are. We infer, therefore, that as the earth is one thing and as we are partly earth and partly something else, this something else is another thing, and further still that in all probability we are a link between these two things which can only consciously manifest in ourselves, but which everthless may exist apart from us as a material and a spiritual world or, when united in perfect equilibrium, form God.

Accepting these possibilities, which are not far removed from the doctrines of the Qabalah, then if any one of us could by some process or another know as much about the spiritual world and its possible spheres of power as we know about the material world, surely such a spiritualized person would possess a stupendous power over his less enlightened fellow men, always granted that there is something spiritual within them. It is the source of this spiritual or magnetic force which we will now enquire into.

The Mystical Ordeal.

There is a spiritual or mystical ordeal, not necessarily order, which all great religious Masters have passed through, and Qabalistically it is fully described in the thirty-second chapter of *Genesis*. [17] In it we read

And Jacob [the *Vau]* rose up that night, and took his two wives [the two *Hehs,* also the pillars of the Temple - Yakhin and Boaz] and his eleven sons [the conjunction of the five and six pointed stars, the Microcosm and Macrocosm; also the *Van* and *Heh* final, which symbolize purification through the balancing of opposites] and passed over the ford Jabbok [the Veil of the Abyss which separates the seven lower Sephiroth from the three Supernal ones]. . . . And Jacob was left alone [in meditation, being cut off from the lower emanations] and there wrestled a man [the ∞*od]* with him until the breaking of the day [the Vision of the *Shin].* And he [the *man - ∞od]* said, Let me go, for the day breaketh [the ∞*od* fearing that if the sun rose, namely the *Shin,* his identity as the potential Tetragrammaton would be lost in the emanation of YHShVH, and his dominion would thus come to an end]. And he [Jacob] said, I will not let thee go, except thou bless me [unite with me, which he can only do through the two wives-the ∞*od Heh* in the seven lower Sephiroth]. And he said unto him, What is thy name?
And he said, Jacob. And he said, Thy name shall be called no more Jacob, but Israel: for as a prince has thou power with God and with men [as above so beneath] and hast prevailed [attained to the spiritual vision].

Jacob then asks of him his name, but the wrestler is silent because his name cannot be pronounced.

And Jacob called the name of the place Peniel, for I have seen God face to face and my life [reason] is preserved.

This ordeal, it will be seen, is of a three-fold nature. First, the aspirant must equilibrate *all* the opposite forces within him, and not merely those he considers vicious. Secondly, he must cut himself away from all outward things and influences and meditate on the Spirit he desires to unite with. Thirdly, he must persevere, that is wrestle with this Spirit. These three acts will lead him to the vision of God, the World Soul, a spark of which burns within him and differentiates him from and also unites him to all things which surround him.

Whilst this vision lasts he is the Messiah, but once it has faded away he is again man, yet charged with a terrific power which according to his will is a power for good or for evil.

The existence and possible employment of this force constitute the great secret of Practical Magic; it is the wand of Thaumaturgy and the Key of black magic. It is the Edenic Serpent who transmitted to Eve the seductions of a fallen angel. The Astral Light warms, illuminates, magnetizes, attracts, repels, vivifies, destroys, coagulates, separates, breaks and conjoins everything under the impetus of powerful wills. God created it on the first day, when He said: "Let there be light." This force of itself is blind but is directed by *Egregores*, that is, by chiefs of souls, or, in other words, by energetic and active spirits. [18]

So writes Éliphas Lévi. These *Egregores* are those who tower above the flock, who are so excellent and distinguished that their wisdom frequently appears to be folly to mankind or else is accepted blindly. The World Fools, or World Sages, attain to something which is extraordinary in its nature and which, when they attempt to reveal it to those unworthy to receive it, renders them magicians, their actions being tinged not only by their mental, moral, and physical characteristics, but also by those of their recipents. Thus we obtain two classes of mysteries or of magic, the white and the black.

The Fourth Dimension.

To the source of mystic power we will now give another name in order to bring it more closely into touch with the ideology of today. We will call it the fourth dimension. Here we have no "up" or "down" in the common meaning of these words; for "up" and "down" are attributes of the threedimensional space in which we consciously live, and to four dimensional consciousness this space and all it contains is nothing more than a mathematical abstraction - a mere notion of the mind.

In spite of the immateriality of the three-dimensional world when viewed from a four-dimensional position, it is possible, as we shall show later on, for a three-dimensional being to establish contact with this source of mystic power, that is to tap it; but once it is tapped it is only possible for the recipient to make use of this power in accordance with his three-dimensional nature. Consequently many of the great religious teachers have insisted on the absolute necessity of their disciples' "purifying" themselves, so that when they attain to the mystic power it may find an equilibrated habitation. For instance, morality, though a gate to the spiritual life, is in no sense its sanctuary; for it is but one of the three great gates - equilibrium of body, heart, and mind. The reason why such innumerable disputes and persecutions have arisen out of the teachings of so many of the Masters is that they have considered morality, and frequently sexual morality, as the only gate and the only end. Misunderstanding the meaning of moral equilibrium, which demands a balancing of all the moral and so-called immoral forces, and not a suppression of any one category of them, they have so completely contorted the three-dimensional medium that when it receives the mystic power a diabolical state is created. Some have gone so far as to command their followers to neglect and macerate their bodies, and others have asserted that the intellect must be annihilated in order to create a vacuum for the onrush of the spirit. The dreadful consequent is that these errors do not prevent attainment; in fact, in many cases they hasten it by cutting down resistance. But what kind of attainment do they lead to? The vision of X, the Unknown God, on entering a balanced medium or body, becomes the Logos; but when it enters an unbalanced body it becomes the Anti-Logos. True, in both cases the fire brought down from heaven is identically the same fire, but according to the medium it inhabits it illumines or blinds.

Those attracted towards this four-dimensional state are such as Éliphas Lévi calls "the energetic and active spirits", that is individuals possessing strong three-dimensional powers - a deep insight into good and evil, the positive and negative currents of life. As beneath, so above; it consequently follows that mundane force is attracted by spiritual force, that the stronger the currents of life the more they are drawn towards the currents of That which created life. And as the mundane force cannot exist without evil, any more than an electrical current can exist without negative electricity, the terrible danger is that spiritual power, like dynamite, can either blast the rock from which the Temple is to be built or blast the Temple which is already built and into which this highest of explosives is off-loaded. Mystic Power is diabolical as well as divine - according to circumstances.

The object of attainment is greater knowledge, understanding, and wisdom of the reality of existence - the Who behind the These. This wisdom in itself cannot assist mankind, though it may utterly change the life of the recipient. It is not the spirituality of the recipient which will tell him how to utilize the power he is charged with, but his intellect h is knowledge, understanding, and wisdom of mankind - that is the mundane shadows of the supernal realities. A physician who discovers some powerful drug would rightly be considered mad were he to administer it to his patients irrespective of their ailments. So also is an adept mad (possessed by Satan) if he attempts to do likewise with his spiritual drug. Worse still, he turns his patients mad and the world becomes a raving hell.

This higher wisdom is a forward impulse of the three-dimensional wisdom, which is a compound of good and evil - the opposite or complementary forces. It is a forward impulse of the will, but with this difference: that whilst in the three-dimensional world a man normally makes use of virtue to enhance virtue and of vice to enhance vice - that is things built upwards - an individual who has experienced the four-dimensional vision, on his re-entering three-dimensional consciousness, sees things *upside down*. Consequently it happens that, unless his intellect has, as in a telescope, been provided with a lens which will reverse the object, he will affirm with all the frenzy of religious faith that the world is standing upon its head. As he knows (three-dimensionally) that the world should stand on its feet, and as he believes (four-dimensionally) that this reversion is necessary to salvation, he will in actual fact turn the world upside down in order to attain his end. To him in his higher wisdom virtue and vice are equivalents, for both are illusions when compared to reality; therefore, according to his nature, he desires to establish reality in the three-dimensional world, and if by nature he is vicious he will attempt to transmute good into evil, and, if virtuous, evil into good. In both cases he will be attempting the impossible. Should he, however, have equilibrated the good and evil qualities of his three-dimensional nature before attaining to the vision of the fourth, knowing that all conscious conceptions are illusionary, after attainment he will remain silent and radiate forth spirituality in place of making graven images of its source.

To will, to dare, to know, and to remain silent are the four supreme powers of the Magus, and the fourth is the divine synthesis of the preceding three. Those who attain to the fourth (the final letter of the divine name) are the leaders of light - the man Jacob who wrestled with Tetragrammaton at the ford of Jabbok and who did not attempt to pronounce his name. Those who attain to the first three only are like Jason, who cast the cubic Stone of the Wise into the midst of the host of warriors (unbalanced forces), who at once turned upon one another in anarchy.

Not one of the great historical religious Masters was a true Messiah; because no man, however sublime may be his nature, can redeem mankind. There is no short cut to heaven, for mankind will find deliverance only when it creates the power which can deliver it; and when it does so, then spontaneously will the Messianic Age be born. Of all these Masters, probably the sublimest was Gotama Buddha, because he refused to discuss the soul, the nature of God, and the joys of heaven. He said: Think rightly, act rightly, live rightly, and deliverance will be revealed to you. He did not say: Accept my thoughts, my words, my life, and salvation is yours. He spoke in parables and locked up the mysteries in his heart; for he understood the sublimity of the true Logos-the Unspoken Word.

CHAPTER VII

THE ANATOMY OF ILLUMINISM

Illuminism.

ILLUMINISM may be defined as "the universal science of light", not only in the spiritual meaning of the words but in their every meaning; for even in its physical nature light is a complete mystery. God is light; out of light is the world created, and out of this formal change appears life, the activity of light whilst death is its shadow or darkness. Between these two stands love, which is light in its human and creative form. In the *Zohar* we read

There is a heavenly David, as well as an earthly one. When God wants to show clemency to the world, He looks at this David, and *His Visage* becomes illuminated. [1]

Here David represents what we have called the fourth dimension; for

whatever is on earth has its counterpart on high, there being no object, however small, in this world but what is subordinate to its counterpart above which has charge of it; and so whenever the thing below bestirs itself, there is a simultaneous stimulation of its counterpart above, as the two realms form on interconnected whole [that is one continuum]. [2]

This world of light is full of symbols, which if we could read them aright would lead us to Reality, which is union with God. There is nothing either created or thought, says Juan de la Cruz, that can offer to the understanding a means suitable for this union; because the understanding is the obstacle which this union has to surmount. Or as the *Zohar* says:

With his ordinary understanding, man cannot understand the revelation of mysteries. All that I am about to reveal to you can be revealed only to the Masters, who know how to keep the balance because they have been initiated. [3]

The physical aspect of illuminism is a definite brilliance of the skin and eyes. We read "Moses wist not the skin of his face shone"; [4] this is not a mere figure of speech. The moral aspect is an irresistible attraction, and the intellectual an overwhelming sense of authority which defies contradiction. Though to the Jews the Messiah represented the Light of the World and his coming meant the conquest of the world, a quite different interpretation was frequently adopted. It was founded upon Jacob's wrestling with Tetragrammaton and it reads as follows:

And he said: Let me go, for the day breaketh. And he said: I will not let thee go except thou bless me. R. Judah discoursed on this verse: *Who is* she *that looketh forth as* the dawn, fair *as* the moon, clear *as* the sun, terrible *as an army with banners?* [S.S. vi, 10.] "This verse", he said, "refers to Israel, at the time when the Holy One, blessed be He, will raise them up and bring them out of captivity. At that time He will first open for them a tiny aperture of light, then another somewhat larger, and so on until He will throw open for them the supernal gates which face on the four quarters of the world. And, indeed, this process is followed by God in all that He does for Israel and the righteous among them. For we know that when a man has been long shut up in darkness it is necessary, on bringing him into the light, first to make for him an opening as small as the eye of a needle [the path of *Daleth* on the Tree of Life] and then one a little larger, and so on gradually until he can endure the full light. It is the same with Israel, as we read: 'By little and little I will drive them out from before thee, until thou be increased, etc.' [Ex. xxiii, 30.] So, too, a sick man who is recovering cannot be given a full diet all at once, but only gradually. But with Esau it was not so. His light came at a bound, but it will gradually be withdrawn from him until Israel will come into their own and destroy him completely from this world and from the world to come. Because he plunged inot the light all at once, therefore he will be utterly and completely exterminated. Israel's light, on the other hand, will come little by little, until they will become strong. God will illumine them for ever." [5]

In short, the Chosen People are the light of the world, a light which at present is mixed with darkness (the Gentiles or children of Esau). This darkness will vanish little by little; first Israel will "look forth as the dawn", next she will "become fair as the moon", then "as clear as the sun", and lastly "terrible as an army with banners". Such is the reformulation of YHVH. When this is accomplished, not a Gentile will be left to pollute the earth; for Israel will have become its Messianic *Shin* which will untie the tongue of God, and on the utterance of His name will the entire universe vanish into absolute light. Such is the inner meaning of illuminism to the Qabalist.

Illuminism and Revolution.

Revolution means turning around. Every twenty-four hours the earth completes a revolution from night to day and back again into night. Man is not so mathematically poised; he cannot calculate the revolutions of his soul. When they occur they come as overwhelming shocks to his whole moral system, and unless he is mentally balanced they are apt to lay him under so tyrannical an obsession that his whole life is thrown out of the perpendicular.

In its psychic form, this problem of revolution is little understood, in spite of the fact that it constitutes the foundation of social evolution and dissolution. When a revolution takes place humanity does not slough its skin; in place its skin is ripped off from it, leaving an agonized body behind. In the past the whole process of deliverance from what is called evil has been so ghastly that it demands our closest attention. Here we will attempt to open its secret chambers.

Light in itself is an invisible vibration which is endowed with visibility by the eye, which in its turn was created by light, that is by countless millions of vibrations playing upon the surface of the living skin until from their irritation was created this most mysterious of all the animal organs of sense. What, then, is mind? Mind, we hazard to answer, is the transmutation of light into thought, that is of spirit into reason. Light is consequently the conductor between divinity and humanity, between God and man. There is the divine thought; there is light; lastly there is human thought: such is the first great psychic, or mystical, revolution.

As man is fashioned from out of inertia, the dust of the earth, and through the breath of life (that is the essence of the divine dynamic) becomes a living soul, his mind (that is the "organ" of his thoughts) is constantly attracted towards inertia. It is only when the God within him, the living soul, is aroused, that he can break away from things earthly and soar closer to the Divine Thought which created him. This breaking away from the inert towards the living is called an act of will – "Let there be light!" but in its restricted human form. Obviously, then, it is a personal endeavour; that is to say, it can only be accomplished by the individual, for though one individual can obtain guidance from another, the toil and the labour is his and his only.

Now the key to the unlocking of the mystery of revolutions, human upheavals, is to be discovered in this word "guidance". If the guide points out the way, leaving it to the free will of the individual to travel along it, then he is a true light unto the guided. But if instead he blindfolds the individual and then forces him in a certain direction, in place of a guide he becomes a tyrant; for in actual fact he will plunge the guided into darkness, a darkness which - though it may take upon itself the appearance of light - is nothing more than a delusion, a dream, and a nightmare. For the individual to will that light shall be is something quite different from being hypnotized into believing that light is and already exists. Belief is of the dust of the earth, it is the static shadow of divine power; will is of the breath of life, it is the dynamic force of that same essence. Thus it happens that true faith is belief crucified on the cross of will, a transmutation of the material into the spiritual. For an individual to accomplish an act of will is to attain to the supreme eucharist; but for an individual to obliterate the wills of others by forcing his will, however spiritualized it may be, on to others is to take part in a black mass. That is to obliterate light, and the higher the spirituality the deeper the darkness resulting.

We will attempt to explain this in simpler terms. If a bright light is brought into a lit room which is crowded with people, it is probable that those nearest to it will blink, but that those at a distance will be but little affected by it. Should, however, the room be in complete darkness, and should those assembled have been in it for a long time, then, irrespective of the conditions of their eye-sight, the probabilities are that all will be blinded and bewildered. Now, if instead of a light an exalted symbol of divinity, a higher idea of God, be explained to a roomful of intelligent and educated people, the influence of this idea is not likely to be great, because they all possess intelligent ideas regarding the Divinity, and consequently these ideas counteract, or drown, the new idea. But if instead the room is filled with uneducated and ignorant people, that is people who having thought little have never developed the critical faculty, then according to the sympathies, antipathies, and emotions of the audience will it accept or reject the idea, not calmly but with frenzy. The idea will in fact detonate a moral explosion.

To turn from the explosive to the exploder, history proves again and again that the greatest religious reformers have almost without exception appealed to the most ignorant and uncultured classes of society. In our opinion these religious reformers never belonged to the higher grade of Masters, because true wisdom reveals that it is madness to attempt to illumine the people *in bulk*; for, though the masses can easily reflect the divine light, they can only do so in an unintelligent way, that is in an anti-divine way, or diabolically. In their case, the intenser the light the profounder becomes the shadow.

We also believe that innumerable attempts to illumine the masses are always being made by Masters of the lower grades, these Masters in the aggregate representing the Satanic force of the world. Further, we know beyond any shadow of doubt that, unless the masses are crude, animal, uncultured, and ignorant, success in transmutation is either wanting or strictly limited. Individuals, like single grains of gunpowder, may be ignited and burn away, but a mass of individuals will not and cannot explode unless through a lack of intellectual freedom it has been tamped into a solid block of powder. In this sense a void is not an emptiness, but a fullness of undifferentiated quality. This is the meaning of the second verse of the first chapter of *Genesis* – "And the earth was without form, and void; and darkness was upon the face of the deep." What did the Spirit of God move upon? "The face of the waters" - that is, an undifferentiated medium, a still and perfect mirror. This was the primal "explosion" which started the revolution of existence. Therefore to detonate revolution there must exist a negative organ and a positive idea; which means that the people must lack intellectual liberty and an illumined Master must exist.

The Fourth-Dimensional State.

From the illumined we will now turn to the illuminator, the man who illumines, and here we will attempt to explain this part of the problem diagramatically.

In Diagram 5 (page 75), AB represents time-space and CD the Divine Spirit which as it impinges on AB creates existence, life, and consciousness. This consciousness grows by a balancing of opposites, the spiritual and the material forces, and once this is realized by man he emerges, or emanates, from his animal chrysalis.

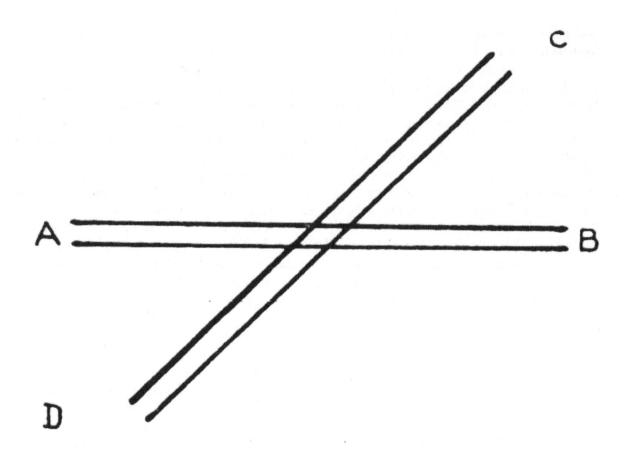

Diagram 5: The Fourth Dimension Diagram 6 is a representation of the Qabalistic Tree of Life in dimensional form. A, D,

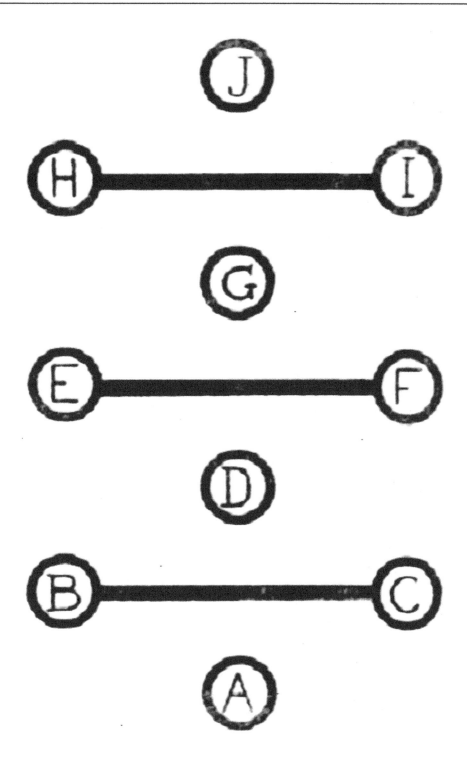

Diagram 6: The Fourth Dimension shown Qabalistically

Diagram 6: The Fourth Dimension shown Qabalistically

G, and J represent the one-, two-, three-, and four-dimensional worlds. The first is cut off from the second by the veil BC, which represents a mathematical point in extension, that is a line - a positive and a negative pole. A dweller in A must penetrate this veil before he can understand what D is like. The second is cut off from the third by the veil EF, which represents length and breadth in extension, that is a plane surface or a line moving outwards from itself. To understand G an inhabitant of D must penetrate EF. The third is cut off from the fourth by the veil HI, which represents length, breadth, and thickness in extension, that is a cube - a plane moving outwards from itself To attain to J consciousness, HI must be transcended.

The scientist, however, insists that there is no separation between G and J, which means that they form a continuum. This may be true enough mathematically, but it is not true in everyday life, for though we recognize time we cannot rationally explain it; it is a mystery, and as great a one as the movement of a point or the movement of a line would be respectively to the dwellers in A and D. To us of three-dimensional consciousness, height or thickness is not a movement, it is a quality of space, something which can be fixed and in abstraction is fixed. Consequently, as time is movement or duration to us, were we to attain to a four-dimensional consciousness it would also become a dimension of space, that is a fixed quality of it, and all spaces lacking this dimension would automatically become mathematical quantities or unsubstantial shadow worlds, pure mental pictures with no real existence outside the mind. Though there may be, and are so mathematically, an infinite number of dimensions beyond the fourth, it is of no consequence to consider them; for ultimately, in order to exist, they must be included - as Bishop Berkeley so sublimely expressed it - in an Eternal Mind or Spirit. Our immediate problem, therefore, is J, and not a".

We will now turn to the upper portion of Diagram 6. The line HI we will suppose separates normal consciousness from abnormal or supernormal consciousness, respectively represented by G and J. The consciousness represented by G is drawn from the experience of the material world, threedimensional space, and that of J is based on experience in the fourth-dimensional world.

The first characteristic of J is that it includes G, and the second that its relationship with G is similar in essence to the relationship between G and D and D and A in Diagram 6. As we have already pointed out, in J all knowledge of G is purely abstract, and so also is all knowledge of J in G; for just as a two dimensional surface of G possesses no thickness and so possesses no tangible reality, so can no part of G possess reality in J. Yet we know that G is real, and consequently from this we infer that J also is real and that their unreality exists only in their relationship, that is in ourselves. This leads us to a fact of some importance, namely, that the reality of J is quite inexplicable in terms of G, except by the means of symbols. Thus, mathematically, it can be inferred that in a four-dimensional world a hollow ball can be turned inside out without breaking its covering; yet it is quite impossible to explain how this is done even if it were actually done before our eyes, because we cannot grasp the fourthdimensional direction.

We will now suppose that X is an ordinary man whose consciousness is expressed in a series of three-dimensional qualities, such as $a^3 + b^3 + c^3 + d^3$ . . . etc.; a representing knowledge, b sentiment, c forcefulness, d sensuality, etc. By some means, which does not here concern us, one day X enters state J (four-dimensional consciousness), whereupon these factors instantaneously become $a^4 + b^4 + c^4 + d^4$ . . . etc. Whilst in state J these factors assume an infinite and absolute character, yet it must not be overlooked that though X on entering J gains a full appreciation of J, his ability to interpret things is limited to his G powers. His mental machinery is still of a G nature, and though all his G factors may be reduced to abstract quantities, his J knowledge is tangible and real and not a mere question of symbols. Whilst in state J he see that a^4, etc., includes a^3, etc., but is infinitely greater, so much so that his G consciousness is entirely swallowed up. For just as a cube contains an infinite number of planes the size of any one of its own sides, so does a^4, etc., include an infinite number of a^3's, etc. Whilst in state J, a^3 etc., sinks into illusion, a^4, etc., becoming the sole reality, which cannot, however, be explained to G individuals in any language they can understand.

The mystical eucharist at an end, X sinks back into state G, and though in this state his sole instrument is his three-dimensional consciousness, the union he experienced was so overwhelming that state J still remains the supreme reality to him. Should he have attained equilibrium in state G before entering state J, he will realize that this is not the only reality; that "as above so beneath", state G is equally real; that they are in fact two realities, the one belonging to conscious existence and the other to what may be called super-conscious existence; that there is a relationship between these two, just as there is a relationship between the human embryo in the womb and the fully developed man; and that to attempt to explain the super-conscious state to the purely conscious individual - that is to an individual who has never experienced super-consciousness - is to turn wisdom upside down.

Such a man, the ordinary individual, we will call Y; then, if X attempts to explain his experiences to Y, as all language deals with three-dimensional concepts, he can only do so by means of symbols, symbols which in some vague way may explain the infinite in terms of the finite and the timeless in terms of the timed. [6]

Should X set out to explain them, to do so he must fall back on his G knowledge and education; consequently his symbols will depend on the relationship between the brilliance he has experienced in J and the balance of knowledge he has established in G - his normal life. The more ignorant he is and the more unbalanced he is the cruder and more unbalanced will his symbols be. He can only build the symbolic temple out of the bricks of his three-dimensional knowledge, and if his mind is of mud and not of clay, then his symbols will be of mud and will never become bricks. The more ignorant he is - that is the less illumined he is in the space world - the darker will be his symbols; consequently should Y be equally ignorant and totally unacquainted with the J vision, and should X force his symbols upon Y (for in spite of his ignorance his experience has endowed him with all the fervour of authority), he will so obsess Y that in place of exalting him to the super-conscious state he will destroy his conscious state and plunge him into a sub- or infra-conscious state. He will. plunge him into the Qliphoth (hell), in which he sees Satan robed in the glory of God. Y will experience a vision of the Devil, the essence of the unbalanced animal Nephesh, and he will be turned upside down. Such is the diagnosis of a would-be white magician creating (unconsciously) a black-magical world.

It is important to enter still deeper into this spiritual devolution. We will suppose that X's predominant characteristic is sentimentality *(b)*, and that it has never been balanced; then the chances are that his symbols will assume a strong b complexion and that in their general form they will become b $(a^3 = a^4)$. Y, we will suppose, becomes magnetized by X's magic; then he will accept the general symbol b $(a^3 = a^4)$ as Reality; but not having experienced what X means by $a^3 = a^4$, when he, magnetized as he is, imposes this symbol on Z, he will not only adulterate it with his own leading unbalanced characteristic, which we will suppose is forcefulness (represented by c), but will do so in a lower degree, that is with lower magnetic power than the degree in which he received it. The general symbol will then become b x c $(a^3 = a^4)$ over 2. Thus the spiritual devolution will continue, and as it rolls downwards it will accumulate more and more unbalanced forces, until it is lost in the nonsense of such a monstrous Hydra-headed symbol as $100a$ x $500b$ x $1100c$ x $300d$ x $900e$ x $700f = (a^3 = a^4)$ over 3600. And as from the very beginning a^3 - a^4 is an absurdity, eventually all spiritual force will disappear, smothered by an accumulation of human desires which draw their strength from the unbalanced primitive instincts and emotions. The symbol will then become an idol.

It will thus be seen that in the search after the Unknowable, God, Super-consciousness - call it what we will - the J state of Diagram 6, the supreme difficulty is not to attain but to explain, and that all explanations, except between beings of equal spiritual *and mundane* knowledge, must lead to the propagation of a lie. The Qabalists are right: the name of God is unpronounceable, and to attempt to pronounce it can only formulate the Devil at the expense of the Divinity. *Diabolus est Deus Inversus* - this is the goal of all false symbols.

The Great Omission.

Having now examined the source of mystic power, which in itself is neither good nor evil, because it is beyond good and evil, but which possessing stupendous energy can accentuate good and evil by potentizing them, we will enquire into the conception of religions and will attempt to ascertain whether, in spite of their astonishing differences, they do not possess some common denominator.

To look for this common factor we must examine the lives of the Masters of religion and not the doctrines of their followers because these doctrines and the activities springing from them consist of a mass of lies and unbalanced movements. Also we must clear our minds of all the worldly sciences - ethics, aesthetics, philosophy, etc. We must jettison the symbolic language of the Masters, and, having swept clean our minds of the dogmas, rituals, and canons of the Churches, we must diligently search for that secret process whereby a helot can be transformed into a hierophant, not magically but spiritually. This indeed is the one and hidden problem of divine alchemy.

We will first examine three Masters known to all - Buddha, Christ, and Mahomet. What is there common in their lives? The first was born a prince; the second was the son of a carpenter - or the son of God if the orthodox object to so humble a parentage; the third was a camel-driver. As different as their origins and worldly occupations were their intellects and characters, and again as different were the religions which they founded. Yet we find one thing in common in the lives of these three men, a blank, a state which we will call "The Great Omission". There is a period in the lives of each of these Masters concerning which nothing is known; for a time each one of them vanished from the world, from public life, and fructified his soul. For several years Buddha sat under the Bodhi Tree, the Tree of Wisdom, meditating on the sorrows of mankind, and there he was transfused with so stupendous a magnetic power that even today his followers number one hundred and fifty millions. Christ, brought up in poverty, from the age of twelve to thirty disappeared from the world, and during this long period no single mention is made of him. Then through baptism and prayer

the heaven was opened, and the Holy Ghost descended in a bodily shape like a dove [symbol of Binah] upon him, and a voice came from heaven, which said, Thou art my beloved Son; in thee I am well pleased. [7]

Today his nominal and actual followers still number six hundred and eighty millions. Mahomet, at the age of thirty-five, retired into a cave and was visited by the angel Gabriel, the Messenger of God; he emerged an illumined adept. His followers conquered half the known world of their day, established a wonderful civilization, and still number two hundred and ten millions.

Is this Omission, this negative period, a coincidence in these three lives? The answer is "no", and this answer is conclusively proved by examining the lives of the lesser Masters. Moses disappeared into the land of Midian, met there seven daughters of the priest of that country, lived with Jethro [8] their father, tended his flocks, led them to the "back side of the desert and came to the mountain of God". "And the angel of the Lord appeared unto him in a flame of fire, out of the midst of a bush." [9] Then he conversed with God, who revealed Himself to be the secret Jehovah; and on his return to Egypt such was his power that not only did he to all intents and purposes found the Jewish religion, but he succeeded in turning Egyptian society upside down. St. Paul journeying to Damascus saw a vision of Jesus Christ, was filled with the Holy Ghost, and retired into the desert of Arabia, and on his return he began to undermine the power of Rome and more than any other man founded Christianity. Simon ben Yohaï, the traditional composer of the *Zohar*, retired with his son to a cave and as legend affirms "sat in the sand up to their necks" for twelve or thirteen years "studying the Law". [10] Also Ramon Lulle, the Qabalist,

In preparing himself for revelation and for the union with God . . . sought the loneliest places and the most arduous ways. He withdrew far from the multitude, where there was nothing to distract him. At the foot of Mount Randa he constructed a little hut in which he received his pupils and taught them. But when he desired communion with God, he climbed to the summit of the mountain. [11]

We will next turn to a modern example, that of Baha u llah, the follower of the Bab. In 1844 the Bab, a young man of twenty-five and the son of a wool merchant, first proclaimed his message in

Shiraz. Seven years later he was put to death at Tabriz and his followers were persecuted for heresy. Baha u llah, a wealthy young Persian of Teheran, became a follower of his, and in the neighbourhood of Baghdad spent eleven years during two of which he hid himself so completely in solitude in the mountains that "his own followers did not know his retreat". On his return his fame soon spread and no attempt to stamp out Babism [12] succeeded.

In Persia itself the persecution that raged intermittently up to the beginning of the present century has been all in vain. The religion grows and grows, silent and unobtrusive like a plant in the dark. [12]

Nor are these mysterious retirements, concerning which the Masters tell us so little, solely connected with religious manifestations for they are to be found in the lives of many of the philosophers. Pythagoras exacted silence and abstinence amongst his disciples for five years; Lao-Tze retired from the world and was inspired of Taoism; Plato enjoined meditation on his pupils; and Bishop Berkeley was wont to retire into solitude at stated periods. Once, writing to a friend, he said

I propose to set out for Dublin . . . but of this you must not give the least intimation to anyone. Speak not, therefore, one syllable of it to any mortal whatsoever. . . . I would have the house with necessary furniture taken by the month . . . for I propose staying not beyond that time and yet perhaps I may. . . . I would above all things have a proper place in a retired situation, where I may have access to fields and sweet air. [13]

Nor does the Great Omission halt here. Abramelin the Magie, a medieval Jewish magician, enjoins retirement. In his book *The Sacred Magic* we are informed:

I resolved to absent myself suddenly, and go away into the Hercynian Forests, and there remain during the time necessary for this operation, and lead a solitary life. [14]

The Mad Mullah of Sudan fame sat in a cave under the Nile and repeated to himself the two-andseventy names of Allah until Allah appeared to him. The Qabalist Hayyim Samuel Jacob Falk, born in 1708, did much the same; an admirer, Sussman Shesnowzi, writes

On one occasion he abode in seclusion in his house for six weeks without meat and drink. When at the conclusion of this period ten persons were summoned to enter, they found him seated on a sort of throne, his head covered with a golden turban, a golden chain round his neck with a pendant silver star on which sacred names were inscribed. Verily this man stands alone in his generation by reason of his knowledge of holy mysteries. [15]

So also did Weishaupt, the supposed founder of the Illuminati, spend five years in meditation (1771-76) and then established his formidable sect. Even Napoleon said:

If I appear to be always ready to reply to everything, it is because, before undertaking anything, I have meditated for a long time - I have foreseen what might happen. It is not a spirit which suddenly reveals to me what I have to say or do in the circumstances unexpected by others - it is reflection, meditation.

Also he said: "I command or I am silent - a profound magical saying.

The Mystic Way.

From the above very brief excursion into the *Zohar* says: "Truly, wisdom is not acquired by a man save when he sits and rests, as it says of Moses that he 'sat on the mountain forty days'." [16] The conclusion is, and this quotation supports it, that normally it is passivity and not activity of mind which unlocks the doors of the mysteries, retirement from the world being the key-hole of the door. Whilst in the passive state, when all mental activities are stilled and the brain itself becomes a spotless mirror, a vision is seen or a voice is heard, and in the twinkling of an eye the whole of man's being is changed and his outlook upon life altered. Modern medical science generally rejects the reality of these visions and classes them under various forms of madness. This explains nothing except that these visions are abnormal.

What is Madness, what are Nerves [cries Carlyle] ? Ever, as before, does Madness remain a mysteriousterrific, altogether *infernal* boiling up of the Nether Chaotic Deep, through this fair-painted Vision of Creation, which swims thereon, which we name the Real. Was Luther's Picture of the Devil less a Reality, whether it were formed within the bodily eye, or without it?

In every the wisest Soul lies a whole world of internal Madness, an authentic Demon-Empire; out of which, indeed, his World of Wisdom has been creatively built together, and now rests there, as on its dark foundations does a habitable flowery Earth-rind. [17]

Both are right, Carlyle in that madness is a mystery, and the doctors in that mystery is often madness to the sane.

The key of passivity has three flanges, namely equilibrium of body, of soul, and of mind. As the Qabalist Isaac Myer says

To arrive at a true knowledge of the simple substances, man must throw off the bond of matter, and by meditation transport himself into the intelligible world, and so seek to identify his essence with that of the higher substances; when in that condition, man does not recognize anything of the world of the senses. In that condition, man will find the evident bodies, in comparison with the intelligible substances, extremely insignificant, and see that the corporeal world is borne by the intelligible world, as if it were a ship on the sea, or a bird in the air. [18]

In this state what we have called three-dimensional consciousness is rendered comatose, and with it a world which is both a reality and an illusion, a tangible thing and a mere reflection. Thus, freed from things earthly, the soul of man expands from what Qabalistically is a negative existence towards a positive existence. Metaphorically speaking, first the soul becomes boundless, because the restrictions are removed; then, as the sides of the elemental pyramid dissolve into illusion, does it become the boundless light, and symbolized as the Microcosmic Shin it beholds the Macrocosmic Shin, whereupon God (the Four-dimensional World) is seen face to face, and the hexagram, the symbol of the Great Work, is formulated.

There are many ways of turning this magical key, and not infrequently it is broken in the turning and with it the mind of man snaps into madness. In the West the Key is often turned by piling symbol upon symbol until three-dimensional thought, so to say, is topped and the spirit is freed. In the East this process is usually reversed, and symbol is taken from symbol until the last vanishes and the spirit is left as the one reality. In the West this science is called Ceremonial Magic; in the East, Yoga. Both these methods of approach, though opposite, are effective; the one is like travelling round a circular road from left to right, and the other from right to left. Yet the first is extraordinarily dangerous. For example, take a fly-wheel: if the object is to stop its motion, either the energy of the engine should be decreased until the wheel ceases to revolve, or its energy increased until through centrifugal force the wheel "explodes". Though this sudden shock will stop the wheel, in all probability it will wreck the engine.

Plato, we believe, was right when he said that

The root-matter of this great knowledge is not to be found in books; we must seek it in ourselves by means of deep meditation, discovering the sacred fire in its proper source. . . This is why I have written nothing concerning these revelations and shall never even speak about them. Whosoever shall undertake to popularize them will find the attempt futile, for, except in the case of a very small number of men who have been endowed with understanding from God to discern these heavenly truths within themselves, it will render them contemptible to some, while filling others with vain and rash self-confidence, as if they were depositaries of marvels which they do not understand all the same. [19]

On the Tablet of Cebes may be read these words:

There is only one real road to be desired, and this is wisdom; there is but one evil to fear, and it is madness.

In these few words are summed up the rewards and the penalties of the Mystic Way. To attain to the Light, the ineffable LVX, is the act of a Magus; to expend this power is the act of a Magician. If held erect, as held by Buddha, so that the uninitiated can see only its reflection, then Magic is White. To hold it downwards so that the light burns among them, then Magic is Black. The first attitude is symbolized by the trident of Neptune, the ruler of the unstable waters; the second by the threepronged fork of the medieval Devil, by which souls are cast into hell. The united trident and fork are symbolized in the double *Shin*, and also in the hexagram or Seal of Solomon or of David.

Like moths the uninitiated circle round these blinding lights and, becoming drunken on their brilliance, are scorched in their fire. As on the physical plane a man can become intoxicated on wine, and on the sensuous on love, and on the intellectual on knowledge, so also in the super-sensuous world can he become drunken on the energy of the spirit. Woe to him who so drinks, for in place of seeing he will become blind. Reeling through the world he will use his trident like a pitchfork, turning humanity upside down. Such a man, as Éliphas Lévi warns us, "is a walking scourge and a living fatality; he may slay or violate; he is an unchained fool".

HEBREW ALPHABET AND CORRESPONDENCES

No.	Hebrew Letters	Latin Equivalents	Name of Letters	Numerical Values	Significations
1	A	A	Aleph	1	Ox
2	B	B	Beth	2	House
3	G	G	Gimel	3	Camel
4	D	D	Daleth	4	Door
5	h	H	Heh	5	Window
6	v	V	Vau	6	Nail
7	z	Z	Zayin	7	Sword
8	c	Ch	Cheth	8	Fence
9	t	T	Teth	9	Serpent
10	y	I	Yod	10	Hand
11	k	K	Kaph	20	Palm of hand
	Final j			500	
12	l	L	Lamed	30	Ox-goad
13	m	M	Mem	40	Water
	Final i			600	
14	n	N	Nun	50	Fish
	Final O			700	
15	s	S	Samekh	60	Prop
16	o	O	Ayin	70	Eye
17	p	P	Pe	80	Mouth
	Final e			800	
18	x	Tz	Tzaddi	90	Fish-hook
	Final f			900	
19	q	Q	Qoph	100	Back of head
20	r	R	Resh	200	Head
21	w	Sh	Shin	300	Tooth
22	u	Th	Tau	400	Cross

GLOSSARY OF HEBREW WORDS AND NAMES

Abbah..Father

Adam Illaah...................................Adam Qadmon

Adam Qadmon ....The Archetypal Man, Heavenly Adam

Adonai..Lord, Tetragrammaton, YHVH

Ain Soph.......................................Eternality of the Ayin

Ain Soph Aur................................Light in vibration, extension of the Ayin

Assiah...World of Action

Atteek ....Holy King

Attikah D'Attikin...........................Ancient of Ancients

Attikah Qadosha ....Sacred Ancient

Atziluth...Archetypal World

Aur ....The equilibrating principle, Light

Awir..Ether

Ayin..No-Thing, Primal Cause, Eye

Be   Raishith.................................Through Wisdom

Binah..Second or third Sephirah, Understanding

B'raishith ....In the beginning

Briah ....World of creation

Boaz ....Black or red pillar of Solomon's Temple

Daath ....Knowledge (not a Sephirah) *Din*

....Judgment, name of Geburah

Dmooth...Divine Resemblance in Lower Manifestation

Douma or Dumah ....Angel of Silence

Dyooknah......................................Shadow of the Divine Phantom Image

Ehyeh ....I am

El..Angel, divine termination

Elohim ....Gods as Nature, "God" in the Bible

Geburah...Fifth Sephirah, Severity

Gedulah...Magnificence, name of   Hesed

Havah..Eve

Hay-yah...Holy Living Creature, the Beast

Hesed ....Fourth Sephirah, Mercy

Hod ....Eighth Sephirah, Glory

Hokmah..Second or third Sephirah, Wisdom

Immah ....Mother

Kether..First Sephirah, the Crown

Maah..What?

Maaseh Merkabah ....Chariot Throne

Macroprosophos............................A name of Kether and of Adam Qadmon

Ma   hshabah ....Thought of the Divinity

Malkuth...Tenth Sephirah, the Kingdom

Matrona ....Name of Malkuth, Matron

Mee..Who?

Metatron..Angel of the Covenant and of Briah

Midrashim.....................................Jewish expository sacred literature

Mishna ....Jewish traditional doctrine

Mitsraim.......................................Egypt

Nachash ....Serpent

Nephesh..Animal vitality, sphere of the emotions

Neshamah......................................Spiritual and Moral Consciousness

Netza'h...Seventh Sephirah, Victory

Ngo..Plague

Ob ....The passive force

Od ....The active force

Ong ....Pleasure

Pahad...Name of Geburah, Punishment

Qabalah ....Oral doctrine

Qliphoth..World of demonic forces, Hell

Ra   ....Evil

Rua   h...Sphere of the reason

Sammael..Angel of Yetzirah, also Lucifer and Satan

Sapheir...To count

Sephirah..Divine emanation

Sephiroth......................................Plural of Sephirah

Shaddai ....God before he revealed himself as YHVH

Shekinah.......................................Presence of the Deity, Glory of God

Sod ....Mystery, Secret

Talmud..The body of Jewish civil and canonical law

Tiphereth......................................Sixth Sephirah, Beauty

Tob...Good

Torah..The Pentateuch or Law of Moses

Tzelem..Phantom of the Divine Image *Tzure*

....Divine Prototype

∞akhin..White pillar of Solomon's Temple

∞eheshuah ....Secret name of Tetragrammaton

∞ehe Aur.......................................Let there be light

∞ehidah...Personality

∞esod ....Ninth Sephirah, Foundation

∞etzirah..World of Formation

∞HVH ....Tetragrammaton, Adonai, Lord, Jehovah

Zohar..Book of Splendour

Zurath...See *Tzure*

REFERENCES

INTRODUCTION

1   *Matthew*, vii, 6.
2   *Acts*, vii, 22.
3   *Numbers*, xi, 24.
4   Aristotle, *De Coelo*, Bk. II, c. 13.
5   Lactantius, *Works*, Bk. III, c. 24.
6   *De Civitate Dei*, St. Augustine, Bk. XVI, c. 9.
7   *Zohar*, III, fol. 10a. (Soncino edition, Vol. IV, p.344.)
8   Origen, *Contra Celsum*, in the Ante-Nicene Christian Library, p.403.
9   *Nachtrag von . . . Originalschriften*, Vol.II, pp. 100-1.
10   *The Kabbalah*, Christian D. Ginsburg, pp. 84-5
11   Translated in the Soncino edition of the *Zohar*.
12   Translated in *The Kabbalah Unveiled*, S. L. Macgregor Mathers.
13   *Ibid.*
14   *Ibid.*

CHAPTER I

1   La Kabbale, p.39.
2   *Ecclesiastes*, iii, 21.
3   *Numbers*, xi, 24 *et seq.* 70 = *Sod*.
4   *Zohar*, III, fol. 152b. (Soncino edition, Vol. V, p.211.)
5   Zohar, II, fol. 99a. (Soncino edition, Vol. III, p.301.) See *The Zohar*, Bension, p.21.
6   *Proverbs*, xxv, 2.
7   *Ibid.*, xi, 2.
8   *Zohar*, I, fol. 28b. (Quoted *The Holy Kabbalah*, Waite, p.306.)

The difference between these two laws is explained as follows: "We read in the Talmud that a Gentile once came to Shamai and said, 'How many laws have you?' Shamai replied, 'We have two, the written law and the oral law'. To which the Gentile made answer, 'When you speak of the written law, I believe you, but in your oral law I have no faith. Nevertheless you may make me a proselyte on condition that you teach me the written law only.' Upon this Shamai rated him sharply, and sent him away with indignant abuse. When, however, this Gentile came with the same object, and proposed the same terms to Hillel, the latter proceeded at once to proselytize him, and in the first day taught him Aleph, Beth, Gemel, Daleth. On the morrow Hillel reversed the order of these letters, upon which the proselyte remonstrated and said, 'But thou didst not teach me so yesterday.' 'True,' said Hillel, 'but thou didst trust me in what I taught thee then; why, then, dost thou not trust me now in what I tell thee respecting the oral law ?' " – *Shabbath*, fol. 31, col. i. (*A Talmudic Miscellany*, by Paul Isaac Hershon, p. 18.)

The significance of this story lies in the fact that God unrolled the universe in the form of the twenty-two letters of the Hebrew alphabet in the order Aleph to Tau, consequently to reverse this order is symbolic of turning the work of God upside down. Therefore, whilst the written law is presumably God-like, the oral law is presumably Satanic. The one creates the world; the other destroys it.

9   *The History of Magic*, Éliphas Lévi, p.46.

10   *Ibid.*, p.138.

11   *The Essenes: their History and Doctrines*, Christian D. Ginsburg, p.12.

12   *The Zohar*, Bension, p. 117.

13   *Ibid.*, p. 117.

14   *Nut* = yolk, *Shu* = white, and *Seb* = shell.

15   *Qabbalah*, Isaac Myer, p. 108.

16   Quoted by Isaac Myer, *Qabbalah*, p. 115.

17   *De Rerum Natura*, Lucretius, Bk. I, pp. 151-265.

18   *Zohar*, II, fol. 100b. (Soncino edition, Vol. III, pp.305-6.).

19   *Comment on Sepher ∞etzeerah*, p. 65. (Rittangel's edition.)

20   *Isaiah*, xlv, 7.

21   *Zohar*, I (Soncino edition), Vol. I, p.6, fol. 2a.

22   *The Zohar*, Bension, pp.210–11.

23   *Ibid.*, p.145.

24   *Ibid.*, p 137.

25   *Zohar*, I, p.6 (Soncino edition), fol. 2a.

26   *Zohar*, I, fol. 156b. (Soncino edition, Vol. II, p.102.)

27   *Ibid.* 28 *Sepher Shepathal*, fol. ii, col. 2.

29   *Matthew*, xviii, 10.

30   *Matthew*, x, 29; *Luke*, xii, 6, 7.

31   *Zohar*, I, p.6 (Soncino edition), fol. 2a.

32   *The History of Magic*, Éliphas Lévi, p.73.

33   *The Zohar*, Bension, p.138.

34   The 72 names of Shemhamphorash.

35   *The Zohar*, Bension, p.137.

36   *Ibid.*, pp.123-4.

37   *Exodus*, xxxiii, 18-23.

38   *Zohar*,   I,   pp.83-4 (Soncino edition), fol. 19b, 20a.

39   *Memorabilia*, Bk. IV, c. 3.

40   *Disp. Tusc.*, Bk. I, c. 28.

41   *Romans*, i, 20.

42   *Acts*, xvii, 28.

43   *Étude concernant la religion populaire des Chinois*, J. J. M. de Groot, Vol. II, p.692.

44   *Asiatic Journal*, No. XXXVI, New Series, Dec. 1832, p. 306.

CHAPTER II

1   *Zohar*, III, fol. 288b. Quoted by Myer, p. 127. (*Ayin* the letter has the value of 70 and is symbolized by the "eye"; 70 = *Sod*, etc.)

2   *Job*, xxvi, 7.

3   *Zohar*, I, fol. 56 (Cremona edition). Quoted by Myer, p.195.

4   *Zohar*, I, p.6 (Soncino edition), fol. 2a.

5   *Ibid.*, I, pp. 110-11 (Soncino edition), fol. 29a.

6   *Sepher ∞etzirah*, Knut Stenring, Chap. I, 1, 2.

7   Sephiroth is plural, Sephirah singular.

8   Zohar, III, fol. 288b. Quoted by Myer, p.127.

9   *Ibid.*, III, 290a. Quoted by Myer, p.193.

10   *Ibid.*, III, 290a. Quoted by Myer, p.199.

11   *Ibid.*, III, 188b. Quoted by Myer, p.200.

12   *Ibid.*, III, 296a. Quoted by Myer, p.201.

13   *Qabbalah*, Isaac Myer, p. 454.

14   *Genesis*, i, 14.

15   I Corinthians, ii, 7, 8.

16   *Colossians*, i, 15-17.

17   *Daniel*, vii, 9.

18   St. John, i, 1.

19   *Zohar*, III, fol. 296a. Quoted by Myer, p.271.

20   *Ibid.*, III, fol. 296a. Quoted by Myer, p.271.

21   Exodus, xxiii, 20–1.

22   *Zohar*, III, fol. 288b. Quoted by Myer, p.259.

23   *Zohar*, I, p.241 (Soncino edition), fol. 71b.

24   *Ibid.*, II, fol. 43a. Quoted by Myer, pp. 328–9.

25   *Qabbalah*, Isaac Myer, p.330.

CHAPTER III

1   *Qabbalah*, Isaac Myer, pp.184-5.

2   *Zohar*, II, p.278 (Soncino edition), fol. 205a.

3   *Ibid.*, II, p.274, fol. 204a. *Beth* is the central letter of Sabbath - *Shin, Beth, Tau*: the 300 emanations of the Yetziratic World, the creative word, and the final 400 emanations of the Assiatic World. Sabbath is creation in harmony.

4   *Zohar*, II, p.190 (Soncino edition) fol. 180b.

5   *Ibid.*, II, p.192 (Soncino edition) fol. 181a.

6   *Ibid.*, II, p.205 (Soncino edition) fol. 184b.

7   *Sepher ∞etzirah*, Knut Stenring, Chap. I, 5.

8   *Ibid.*, Chap. II, 4.

9   *Qabbalah*, Isaac Myer, p.185.   10 *Mishna*, II, vi.

11   *Zohar*, II, p.21 (Soncino edition), fol. 131a.

12   *Zohar*, I, 35a (Amsterdam edition). Quoted by Myer, p.345.

13   *The Kabbalah*, Christian D. Ginsburg, p.111. See also *Zohar*, II, fol. 255 - 9, and I, fol. 35b.

14   *Etz ha-Hay-yem* (Tree of Life), fol. 253, col. 2.

15   *Qabbalah*, Isaac Myer, p.331.

16   Quoted from *The Holy Kabbalah*, A. E. Waite, p.447.

17   *N.B.* the first and last letters of the alphabet united by the mystic *Shin* - Sh.

18   Also called Chayoh, Hay-yoth, and sometimes Chiva.

19   As marriage was a sacred act, prostitution was a diabolical act. The union between man and woman is opposite to that between the lower animals, hence the degrading name of "Beast".

20   *History of Magic*, Éliphas Lévi, p.192.

21   *Zohar*, I, Appendix III, Mathnitin; II, 105. The numerical value of Shaddai and Metatron is 314. Myer, p. 366.

22   In the trump cards of the Tarot, the card marked *Aleph* shows a Fool (Supreme Intelligence) followed by a hound (Satan) or inferior intelligence.

23   *Sepher ∞etzirah*, Knut Stenring, Chap. III, 10.

24   *Ibid.*, p. 66. 25 This figure combines the value of *Shin* = 300 and of *Sod* (Mystery) = 70. The 706 also refers to the 70 nations of the world.

26   Quoted from *Qabbalah*, Isaac Myer, p.234.

27   *Ibid.*, pp. 186-7

28   *Zohar*, I, p.110 (Soncino edition), fol. 29a.

29   *Ibid.*, I, p. 177, fol. 55b.

30   *Ibid.*, II, p.213, fol. 186b-7.

31   Quoted from *Qabbalah*, Isaac Myer, p.110.

32   *Zohar*, II, p.375 (Soncino edition), fol. 244a.

33   *Ibid.*, II, p.375, fol. 244a.

34   *Ibid.*, I, pp. 105-6, fol. 27b. By "mixed multitude" is meant "Gentiles".

35   *Ibid.*, II, p. 197, fol. 182a.

36   *Ibid.*, III, fol. 260b (Pauly edition).

37   *Ibid.*, I, fol. 14a.

38   *The Secret Doctrine of Israel*, A. E. Waite, p.241.

39   *The Kabbalah*, Christian D. Ginsburg, pp. 120-1.

CHAPTER IV

1   *The Zohar*, Ariel Bension, p.37.
2   *Zohar*, I, pp.67-8 (Soncino Edition), fol. 16a.
3   *The Zohar*, Ariel Bension, p.132.
4   *Ibid.*, p.133.
5   *Zohar*, III, fol. 128a. See Myer, p. 127. See also *Midrash* (Bereshith Rabba), Section IX (Pauly edition). 6 *Ibid.*, II, fol. 110b.
7   *Ibid.*, III, fol. 292b. See Myer, p.386.
8   *Ibid.*, II, fol. 20a.
9   *Ibid.*, III, fol. 142a. Also III, fol. 290a. See Myer, p.199.
10   *Qabbalah*, Isaac Myer, p.418.
11   *Genesis*, ii, 7.
12   *Zohar*, I, p.101 (Soncino edition), fol. 26a.
13   *Ibid.*, I, fol. 205b (Brody edition).
14   *Qabbalah*, Isaac Myer, p.392.
15   *Zohar*, I, p.83, and II, p. 150 (Soncino edition), fol. 19b and 169b.
16   *Ibid.*, I, fol. 119a (Pauly edition).
17   *Ezekiel*, xxxvii, 22.

CHAPTER V

1   *Genesis*, ii, 7. The *Shin* breathed into YHVH - the four elements.
2   There are three rivers, the Neshamah, Rua h, and Nephesh, the combined essences of which mystically form the fourth river - the Yehidah. The rivers of Eden are Pison, Gihon, Hiddekel, and

Euphrates. The rivers of Hades are Phlegethon, the positive spiritual power; Acheron, the negative spiritual power; Lethe, forgetfulness; and Cocytus, silence. Magical silence leads to worldly forgetfulness, which is attained by equilibrating the negative and positive spiritual forces.

3   *Genesis*, iii, 5. 4

The reader will remember that wc n 50+8+300 (Serpent), = cywm = 40 + 300 + 10 + 8

(Messiah) 5 *Genesis*, iii, 16

6 *Ibid.*, iii, 22-4. 7 The Kerub of Earth is the Bull - the generative principle. In the Mithraic rites, still continued today in the form of the Spanish bull-tight, the drops of blood issuing from the flanks of the dying Beast (666) are the ten ∞odin or Sephiroth of the Tree of Life. The blood and water gushing from the side of the dying Christ are a somewhat similar conception. They symbolize the opposites, good and evil, flowing out of the expiring Assiatic world.

8   The numerical value of ∞od, *Heh*, *Shin*, *Vau*, *Heh* is 326, which figures if added together equal 11. Eleven is symbolic of the accomplishment of the Great Work, the union of the 5 and the 6, the *Heh* and the *Vau*, the Microcosm and the Macrocosm, the pentagram and the hexagram. The numerical value of Messiah (see above, reference[4]) is 358. These figures added together equal 16, and 1+6=7. Seven added to 11 is i8, and 18 is 6 + 6 + 6, or if 11 is reduced to 2 (i.e. 1 + 1) then 2 + 7 = 9. Nine above and 9 below = 18, and 18 = 6 + 6 + 6.

9   The Messianic mystery was considered so potent that the bulk of it has never been divulged, and still lies hidden away in numerical values. Thus Messiah can be reduced to the value of 7; so can Shekinah (hnykw) so can,

hlyw aby "Shiloh shall come" (*Genesis*, xlix, 10) "and unto him shall the gathering of the people be"; so can "the Tree of Good and Evil".

10   *Genesis*, iv.

11   *Ibid.*, vi, 2.

12   *Ibid.*, vi, 4.

13   *Ibid.*, ix, 21. See also Zohar, 1, p.249 (Soncino edition), fol. 73b.

14   *Ibid.*, xi, 4.

15   *Zohar*, I, p.254 (Soncino edition), fol. 75a.

16   *Zohar*, I, p.254, fol. 75a.

17   *The History of Magic*, Éliphas Lévi, p.454.

CHAPTER VI

1   *The Mysterious Universe*, Sir James Jeans, p.77

2   *Ibid.*, p.141.

3   *Ibid.*, p.78.

4   *Ibid.*, p.132.

5   *Ibid.*, p.121.

6   *Ibid.*, p.137.

7   *Ibid.*, p. 127.

8   *The Expanding Universe*, Sir Arthur

Eddington, p.46.

9   *Ibid.,* p.47.

10   *Ibid.,* p.57.

11   *Ibid.,* pp.103-4.

12   *Ibid.,* p.75.

13   *Ibid.,* p.77.

14   *Ibid.,* pp. 118, 126.

15   *Ibid.,* p.119.

16   *Ibid.,* p. 125. 17 The thirty-second path of the Tree of Life is attributed to the twenty-first Tarot trump - the Universe, on which is depicted a naked woman with a veil drawn over her generative organ. She is placed between the four elemental Kerubim - hvhy The thirty-first path is that of w -the Angel. Though

probably   a
coincidence,
it   is   an
interesting
one.

18 *The History of Magic*, Éliphas Lévi, p.17.

Chapter VII

1 *The Zohar*, Arid Bension, p. 180.

2   *Zohar*, II, p.102 (Soncino edition), fol. 156b.

3   *The Zohar*, Ariel Bension, p. 117.

4   *Exodus*, xxxiv, 29.

5   *Zohar*, II, pp.151-2 (Soncino edition), fol. 170a.

6   a^4 knowledge may not in Reality be infinite, for as far as we know there may be an a^5 or a^6 or a^n knowledge; nevertheless in the realm of the states, or planes, a^4 is infinite when compared to a^3.

7   *Luke*, iii, 22, and Matthew, iii, 16, 17. The Holy Ghost is the triune principle in God, the letter *Shin* which expands Tetragrammaton into Yeheshua. The descending dove represents the *Shin*, the points of the wings and the tail symbolizing the three tongues of flame.

8   The seven daughters are probably the seven lower Sephiroth and Jethro the Supernal triad. 9 *Exodus*, iii, 2.

10   The legend concerning this retirement is a strange one. Prior to A.D. 161 Simon ben Yohai was sent as a delegate to Rome. There he cast out from the Emperor's daughter an evil spirit by name of Ben Temalion. He fell into disfavour, and to escape from the sentence imposed on him by Lucius Aurelius Verus, co-regent of the Emperor Marcus Aurelius Antoninus, he dwelt in a cave. There he and his son were miraculously fed by a carobbean tree and were visited by a Bath Qol (a Holy Guardian Angel). During thirteen years (13 is the value of AChD, Achad, which means unity) he was endowed with a "heavenly superiority and sublimity". See *Qabbalah*, Isaac Myer, pp. 18-23; *A Hebrew Miscellany*, Paul Isaac Hershon, pp. 64-6; and *The Zohar*, Ariel Bension, pp.63-4.

11   *The Zohar*, Ariel Bension, p.63. 12 Babism "accepts Christ in His entirety, without seeking to explain Him away. It says that all the religions of the world are true, but that the teaching of their founders in time becomes obscured; that the world needs a restatement, suited to the needs of the age, of the one great truth which has never varied". "Pilgrims in the Holy Land" - *The Times*.

13   Bishop Berkeley's *Collected Works*, Vol.111.

14   *The Book of the Sacred Magic*, edited by Liddell MacGregor-Mathers, p.25.

15   Quoted by Nesta H. Webster, *Secret Societies*, p. 186.

16   *The Zohar*, II, p.317 (Soncino edition), fol. 223a.

17   *Sartor Resartus*, Chap. VIII.

18   *Qabbalah*, Isaac Myer, p.151.

19   Quoted from *The History of Magic*, Éliphas Lévi, p.136.

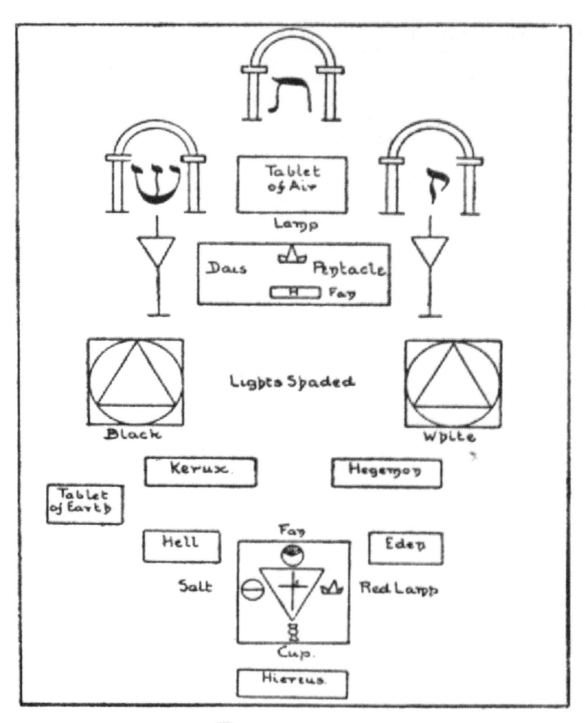

DIAGRAM 20.

Arrangement of Temple for the 32nd Path in the 2° = 9° Ritual.

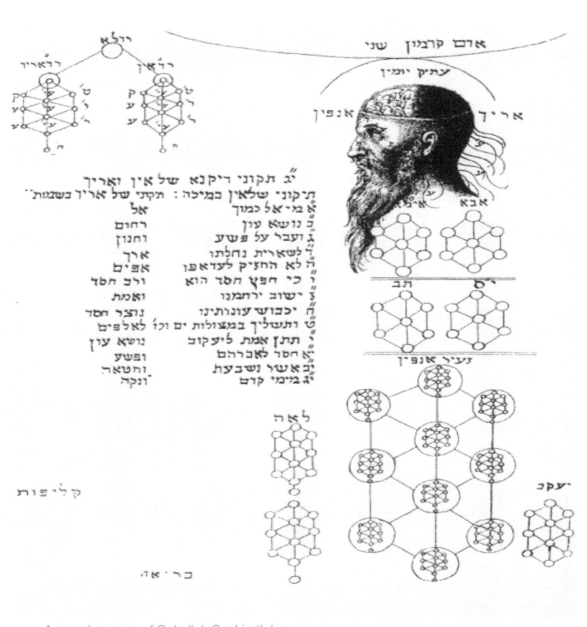

A complex array of Qaballah Sephiroth by
Christian Knorr von Rosenroth, 1684

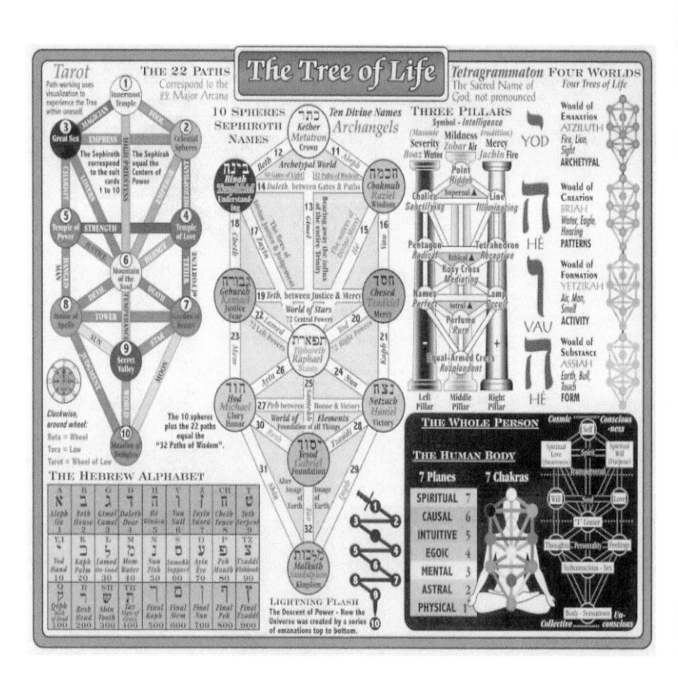